WARWICK

A POTTED HISTORY

LYNNE R. WILLIAMS

AMBERLEY

First published 2026

Amberley Publishing
The Hill, Stroud
Gloucestershire, GL5 4EP

www.amberley-books.com

ISBN 978 1 3981 2941 2 (print)
ISBN 978 1 3981 2942 9 (ebook)

British Library Cataloguing in Publication Data.
A catalogue record for this book is available from the British Library.

Typesetting by Hurix Digital, India.
Printed in Great Britain.

Appointed GPSR EU Representative:
Easy Access System Europe Oü, 16879218
Address: Mustamäe tee 50, 10621, Tallinn, Estonia
Contact Details: gpsr.requests@easproject.com, +358 40 500 3575

Contents

Introduction

What influenced the development of Warwick? Delve into its history and discover amazing stories of dark deeds and disasters. *Warwick: A Potted History* is a fascinating and informative overview together with anecdotal evidence that sheds light on the lives of its people. Following a chronological timeline, Warwick's history is unfolded in three major parts, drawing together threads charting its progress through the ages from its beginnings as a small humble town with a slow-growing economy to a flourishing county and market town.

Long before the establishment of the castle, communities existed in Neolithic and Anglo-Saxon times, as evidenced by excavation finds. Small as it was, Warwick was overrun by warring tribes on six occasions, twice sacked by the Danes. Swathes of territory captured by these fierce Norsemen were retaken by Eric and Ethelfleda, warrior son and daughter of Alfred the Great, under Danelaw, and defensive 'burhs' were established across the country. One such 'burh' was established beside a weir by Ethelfleda called *waering wic*.

The Anglo-Saxon name *waering wic* was to become Warwick. Integral to Warwick's defence, development and importance as a county town is the magnificent castle and its earls. Since it was established by William the Conqueror in 1068, the castle has stood as a monument to Warwick's changing face, from humble beginnings to a thriving market and county town. The castle and its earls have in medieval times acted as a bastion against rebellion to the Crown. As a venue for visits of royalty, the castle has conferred prestige on Warwick and assured its place of importance in the country. Its many earls have played a pivotal role in the town's development politically, socially and economically. From feudal lords honing their skills on the battlefield to town civic influencers and benefactors, these have made a significant impact on the history of Warwick.

A journey through Warwick's history uncovers great events like the visit of Elizabeth I in the sixteenth century, the Great Fire of 1694, the role of the castle during the Civil War, two world wars, the Pageant of 1906 and the replanning of Warwick town by Patrick Abercrombie following the Second World War. Fairs, markets, trades and customs are all part of its rich tapestry woven through history along with crime and punishment.

The population of Warwick has grown substantially from the time of Domesday in 1087 given as 1,500, to 37,000 at the present time, indicating that Warwick is a popular place to live. Over time its fortunes have sometimes dipped but businesses continue to be attracted to the town, contributing to its affluence and prosperity, while the castle has in recent times been an economic benefactor to the town by attracting tourism.

From a once compact and contained town surrounded by fields, farmland and parkland, Warwick has mushroomed substantially. The spread of urban density and loss of its green cloak perhaps detracts from its character as a once small market town.

PART I

In the Beginning – A Small, Humble Town

Way back in the mists of time Neolithic cultures arrived in France, Belgium and Germany, around 1,000 years before they arrived in Britain. It is likely they migrated from Turkey and Greece as farmers. They eventually arrived in Britain after the Mesolithic Britons who inhabited the land bridge known as Doggerland connecting Britain with Europe. A study of the DNA of six Mesolithic Britons and sixty-seven Neolithic Britons by Dr Tom Booth and the British Museum team revealed that most of the hunter-gatherer population was replaced by those carrying ancestry originating in the Aegean.

A Neolithic community was established in Warwick, as shown by excavations in 1966 during the construction of a new bus interchange in the vicinity of Puckering's Lane/Market Street. This recorded evidence dating from the earlier Neolithic occupation to the present day, a span of at least 5,500 years. Early Neolithic evidence consisted of a pit group which yielded pottery, worked flint and hazelnut shells.

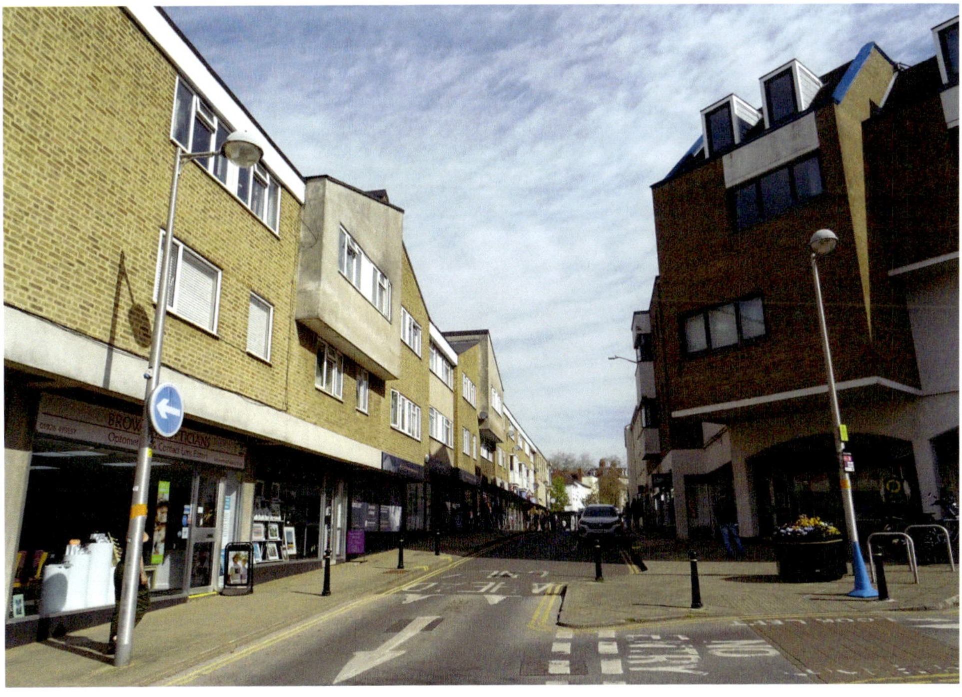

Puckering's Lane junction with Market Street, site of excavation of Neolithic finds in 1966.

With its origins in the Neolithic age, Warwick boasts a long, rich and colourful, occasionally bloody history. The seventeenth-century historian Sir William Dugdale recorded the myth that King Cymbeline founded Warwick in around 5 BC, building the first stronghold that existed on the site of the castle. Contrary to this, the Anglo-Saxon Chronicle states that Aethelflaed, Lady of the Mercians, first founded a fortress at Warwick in AD 914, and this is where our journey through Warwick's history begins.

Occupying a good vantage point on a knoll beside a river crossing, its strategic site wasn't exploited until a warrior daughter of the king determined to recapture territory held by the Danes. A Saxon town sacked and destroyed on no fewer than six occasions, twice by the fierce Norsemen, was fortified in AD 914. Ethelfleda, indefatigable daughter of King Alfred the Great, whom legend says famously burnt the cakes, militarised Warwick by creating a permanent garrison charged with the duty of guarding the 'burh'.

Earthworks were roughly piled up on the site of a mound on the banks of the River Avon, derived from the Welsh Afon, where a natural weir formed a crossing, giving the town its Saxon name of waering, signifying a dam/weir and wic, fortification or farm. However, excavations in 1923 found evidence of two Anglo-Saxon cemeteries. It is thought that there had been a continuous settlement since the sixth century. Graves were discovered at Emscote on the right bank of the River Avon 1 mile above Warwick and 50 yards from the south side of the embankment of the Great Western Railway. The weapons and ornaments unearthed pointed to a flourishing community at that time.

Although it was previously thought the Romans did not occupy Warwick, as they were located further south-east on the Fosse Way, signs of Roman occupation were recently revealed. An archaeological dig on Banbury Road in October 2021, site of the relocation of King's High School for Girls, uncovered the remains of a second-century AD Roman villa. The building showed agricultural use with corn drying ovens and a suite of domestic rooms where the Romans would sleep and eat. It is thought the building probably fell out of use in the fourth-century AD. Other signs of Roman occupation were also found with an archaeological dig in 2004 on the site of the medieval Leper Hospital which unearthed a Roman coin. This was of Faustina II, wife of Marcus Aurelius, and dated from around AD 175.

Roman and Anglo-Saxon occupation of Warwick was superseded by the Normans following the Norman Conquest of England in 1066. This saw William the Conqueror establish a timber fortification on the motte in 1068 and its strategic position was used to defend the Midlands against rebellion from the north. The knoll on which the initial castle was built is an outlier of the Keuper sandstone outcrop and provided a good defensible area on which to build a fortification. It was also to provide a good source of building stone and well water. Ethelfleda's Mound, which still exists today, was said to be the first fortification on the site established in AD 914 as Anglo-Saxon; however, the origins of the mound are thought to be Norman rather than Anglo-Saxon.

Although Warwick already existed as a borough by the time of Domesday, it was shortly afterwards that the Crown granted it to the Earls of Warwick. This was to have ramifications as it was probably due to its high degree of dependence on the earls coupled with economic backwardness that may explain its failure to win or even seek a greater measure of self-governance. The administrative affairs were carried out by three of the earl's officials: the Steward, Bailiff and Rent-collector.

The custody of the castle was first given to Henry de Beaumont who was rewarded for his loyalty by William II in 1088 and created the first Earl of Warwick. Since that time Warwick Castle has been the seat of the Earls of Warwick for many centuries and these have played a central role in the town's defence, development and importance as a flourishing county town.

When Henry of Anjou arrived in England in 1153, the garrison was tricked into handing over the castle, possibly at the instigation of the Countess Gundred in the absence of the earl. He supported King Stephen, Duke of Normandy during his reign known as the 'Anarchy'. It is said he died of vexation on hearing the news.

The timber-built construction was fortified in the twelfth century with stone and over time its defences were further strengthened with the additions of Guy, Caesar's, Bear and Clarence Towers. The living quarters were extended and embellished and the grounds transformed. The demolition of cottages in the immediate neighbourhood enabled the castle to be extended by its earl, George Greville, in the eighteenth century.

Guy and Caesar's Towers, built in the fourteenth century, were the most formidable defences and Bear and Clarence Towers represent the remains of a fifteenth-century fortification. The central part of the castle includes the Great Hall and State Rooms and represent the living quarters of the castle in the fourteenth century; however, little of its medieval structure now remains. Alterations were carried out in the seventeenth and eighteenth centuries to extend at both ends and towards the courtyard.

At the time of Domesday in 1087 Warwick was recorded as a burgh possessing 225 houses, once guarded by a ditch. The fifteenth-century historian John Rous writes of

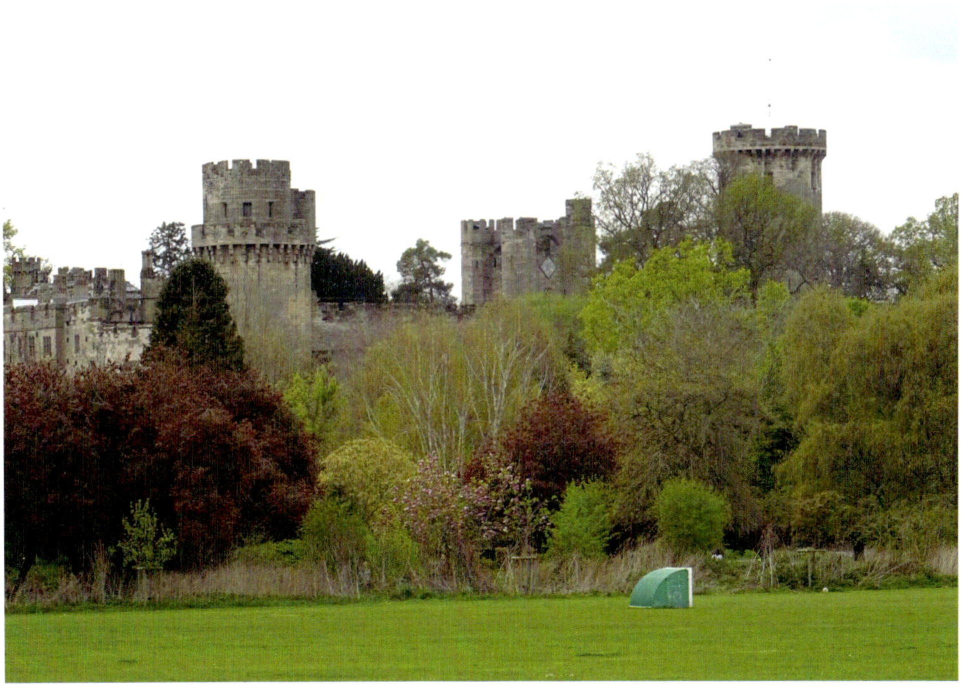

Caesar's and Guy's Towers, constructed in the fourteenth century.

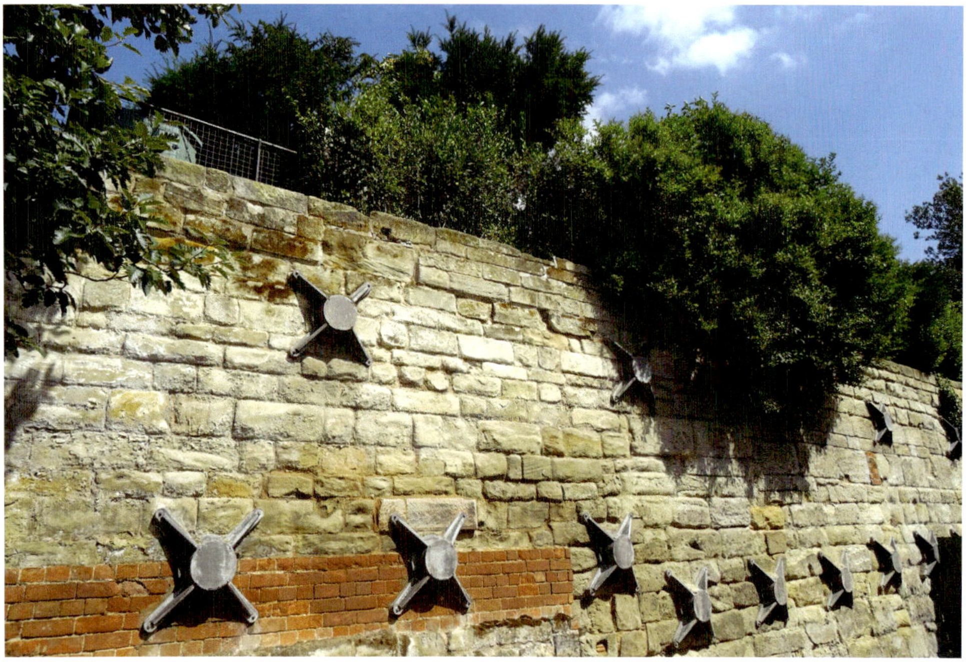

Remains of the original town wall in Bowling Green Street.

a great defensive ditch made by Turchil of Arden, a Saxon vassal of the Conqueror. The population at that time was 1,500. To enhance defences of the town, north, east and west gates were constructed together with a boundary sandstone wall. Part of the wall exists today in Bowling Green Street and provides the boundary to the gardens of the Lord Leycester Hospital. With the town now encircled, Warwick could look forward to a secure and prosperous future.

Westgate, constructed in the twelfth century, was a combination of chapel and tollhouse. A formidable entrance to the town with a ribbed, barrel-vaulted ceiling was described as a 'hanging gate'. St James' Chapel over the archway was granted to the Guild of St George the Martyr in 1353 by Thomas Beauchamp, Earl of Warwick. The gateway was extended under the chapel and a tower added in 1450.

Adjacent to Westgate is the medieval Guild buildings forming the Lord Leycester Hospital, which was licensed by Robert Dudley, Earl of Leicester in 1571, providing a home for twelve old and disabled soldiers. The term hospital was used in its ancient sense meaning 'a charitable institution for the housing and maintenance of the needy, infirm or aged'. These are still occupied today by the 'Brethren' who regularly attend service in the chapel of St James wearing their traditional black gowns with the bear and ragged staff insignia, and Tudor hats.

Ralph Griffiths was the first master, followed by Thomas Cartwright in 1584. His appointment was seen as part of a concerted and wily plan by Dudley and brother Ambrose, Earl of Warwick to strengthen the Puritan cause in Warwickshire. Prior to his appointment, Thomas Cartwright had been imprisoned for promoting his Puritan beliefs and only released after Robert Dudley interceded on his behalf with Elizabeth I.

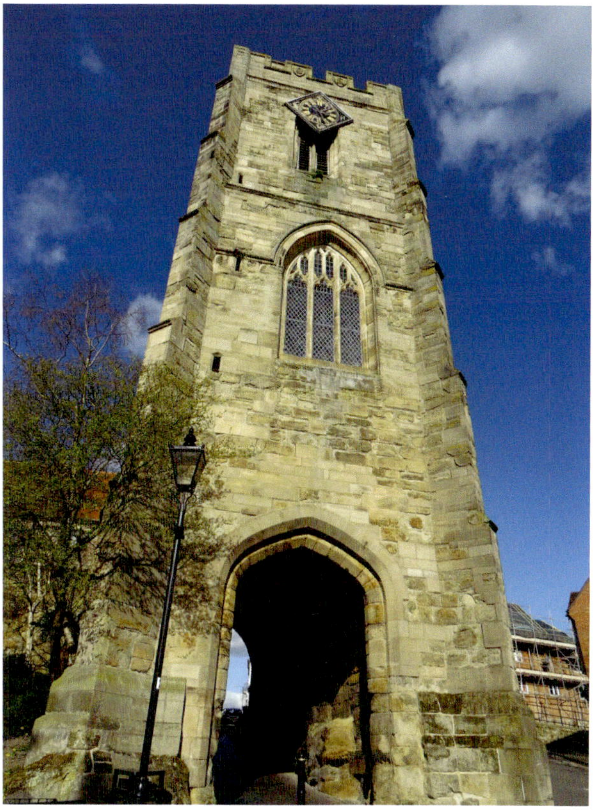

Right: Westgate, a Grade I stone-ribbed barrel-vaulted archway dating back to the twelfth century, was one of the three gates into the town.

Below: Ribbed barrel vaulting, Westgate Arch.

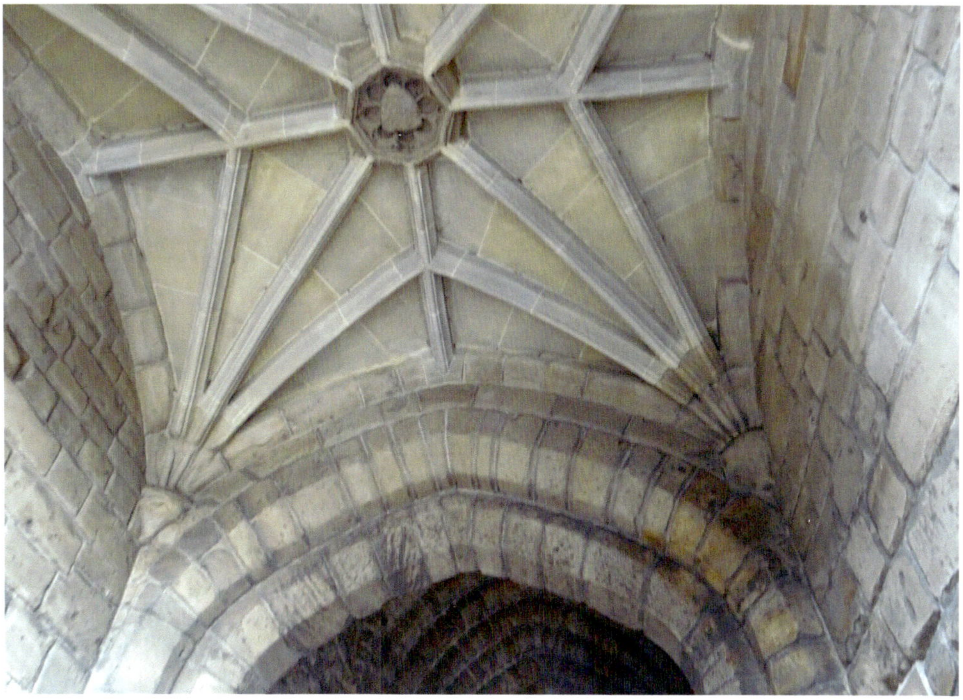

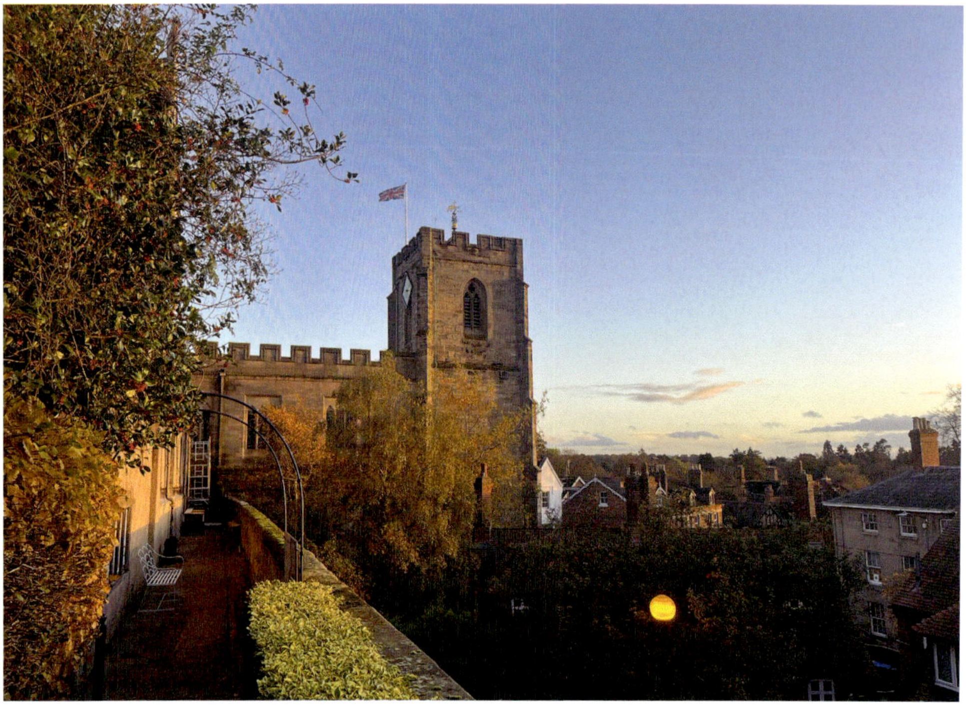

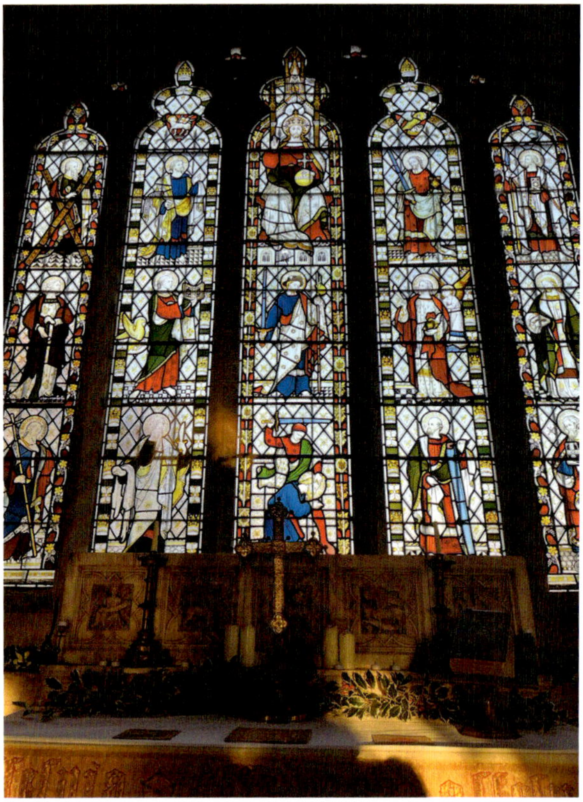

Above: St James' Chapel above Westgate Arch was built by Roger de Newburgh, Earl of Warwick in 1123 as a chantry chapel. After falling into disrepair, it was rebuilt by Thomas Beauchamp in 1383 and gifted to the Guild of St George by King Richard II. Adjacent to the chapel is part of the remains of the old town wall, boundary to the Lord Leycester gardens. (Image by kind permission of The Lord Leycester)

Left: Stained-glass window in St James' Chapel – the work of Birmingham firm Clayton & Bell, designed by William Morris and depicting Christ as Salvator Mundi with fourteen of his saints. (Image by kind permission of The Lord Leycester)

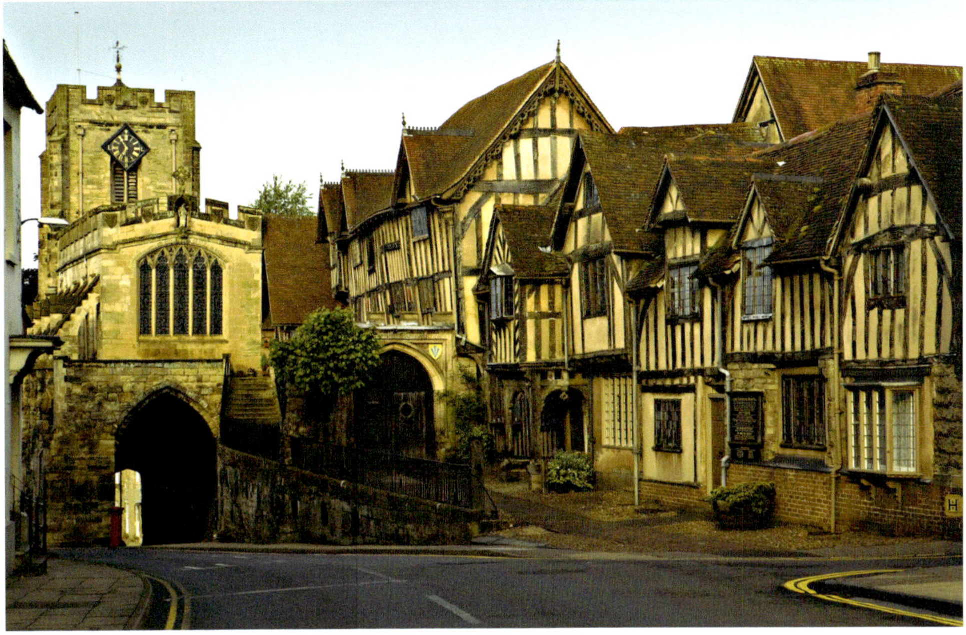

The Guild buildings were licensed by Robert Dudley, Earl of Leicester in 1571 who established a hospital for twelve old and disabled 'Brothers' and a Master. (Image by kind permission of The Lord Leycester)

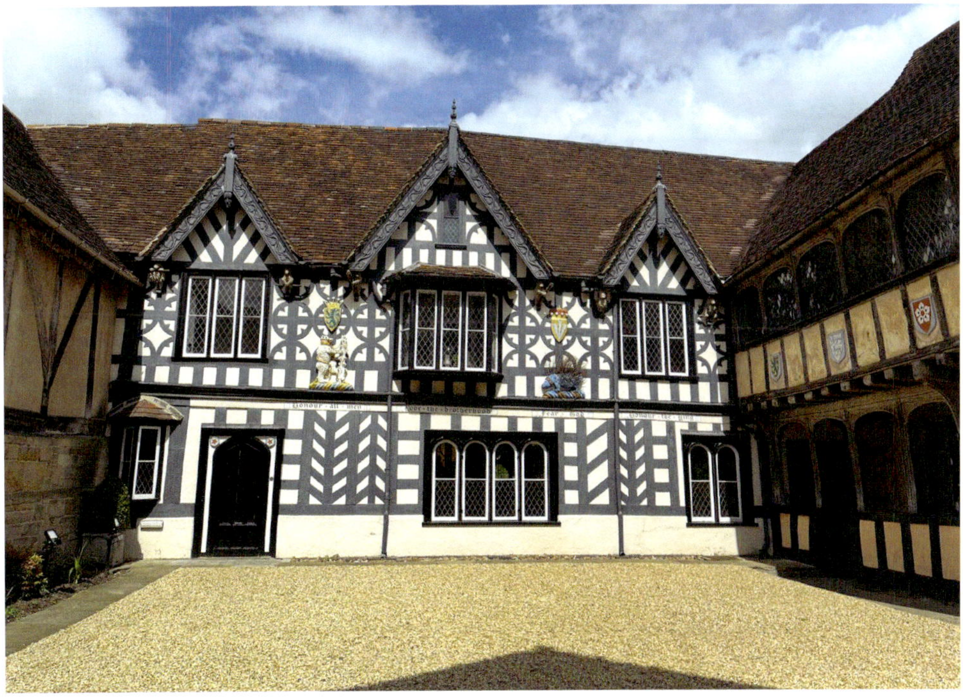

The east and south aspects of the Lord Leycester courtyard. (Image by kind permission of The Lord Leycester)

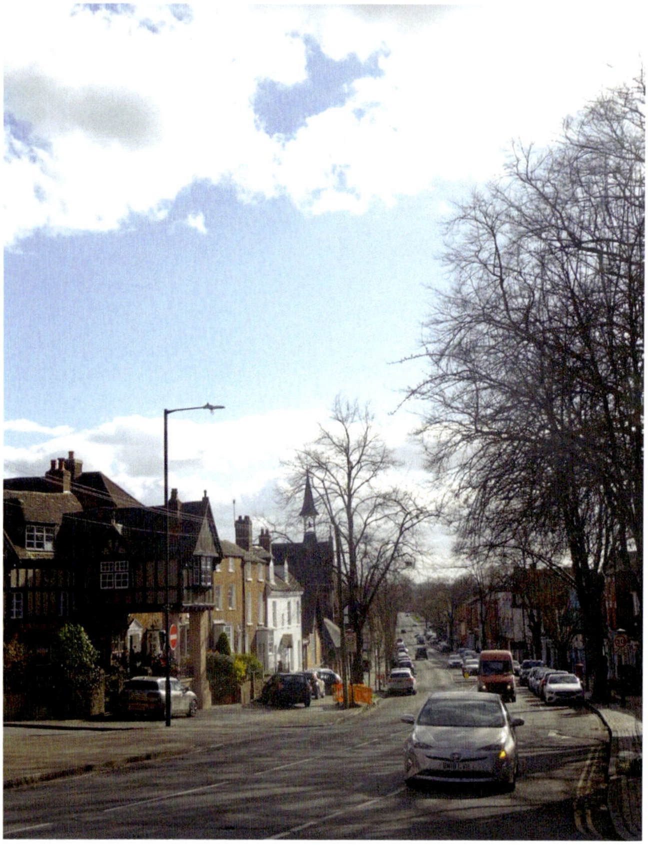

West Street – part of the western suburb of Warwick where horses and ponies were sold during the nineteenth century; also, the location of thirteenth-century St Lawrence's Church, now demolished.

The appointment of the Master was to be made by the earl and his heirs, and the Master and Brethren became a corporate body. The death of the Earl of Warwick in 1590, who died without an heir, deprived the hospital of its protector, threatening its continuation. Lettice Knollys, widow of Robert Dudley, tried to claim Lord Leycester Hospital's lands for herself and only the intervention of Lord Burghley, Lord High Treasurer, at the urgent request of Thomas Cartwright, saved it. King James I granted titles and favours to Dudley's nephew, Robert Sidney, and the Sidney family remain the hereditary patrons of the Lord Leycester Hospital to this day.

Beyond Westgate the western suburb comprised of West Street, Walkers Lane and Queenwell Street (Friar Lane) where the Dominican Friary was situated, close to an area of common pastureland called Clay Pits. This was first established towards the end of the reign of Henry III. Timber was granted for it in 1263, and a church was built by 1268. The Black Friars were so called because of the colour of their cloaks.

History of the County of Warwick: Volume 2 records that Henry III granted a special favour to the friars on 4 March 1267. He directed a mandate to all bailiffs and other officers on their route to permit the friars to carry their herrings and other victuals freely from Norwich without any toll or other hindrance until the following Easter. As their staple diet during Lent was salt herring, this exemption from a toll was of real benefit to them.

Under Henry VIII's Dissolution of the Monasteries, Thomas Norman, the Prior, and seven friars signed the surrender of their house and possessions to Dr London on 20 October 1538. Dr London suggested that the roof of the friary, being 60 feet long, with good tiling would serve for the kitchen that the king was building at Warwick Castle. The Prior and his 'brethren' were ejected like the rest of the friars without a pension.

Our Warwickshire records that the site was purchased by John, Duke of Northumberland in 1551, who held it long enough to demolish the church and building. Excavations of the Black Friars Monastery located somewhere opposite St Paul's Church revealed pieces of stained glass and five pieces of human bones in 1835. Further human remains, animal bones and pottery were also excavated in 1973 and are now held in Warwick Museum.

Also situated in West Street outside the town walls was the medieval thirteenth-century Church of St Lawrence. The building was recorded as still standing in 1632. When the road was widened in 1837 a churchyard was discovered and a Norman capital was found. This was part of Norman architecture where semi-circular arches were mounted on pillars topped with either plain or finely sculptured capitals. Excavations revealed an aisle on the north side and a chancel. The church had also been used as a barn for a short period.

The northern gate referred to in 1272 has long since been demolished. This is thought to be in early Tudor times, as it had disappeared by the time the traveller John Leland arrived in Warwick in the first half of the sixteenth century. Leland records he saw the remains of the town wall near the west and east gates. The only remaining stretches of

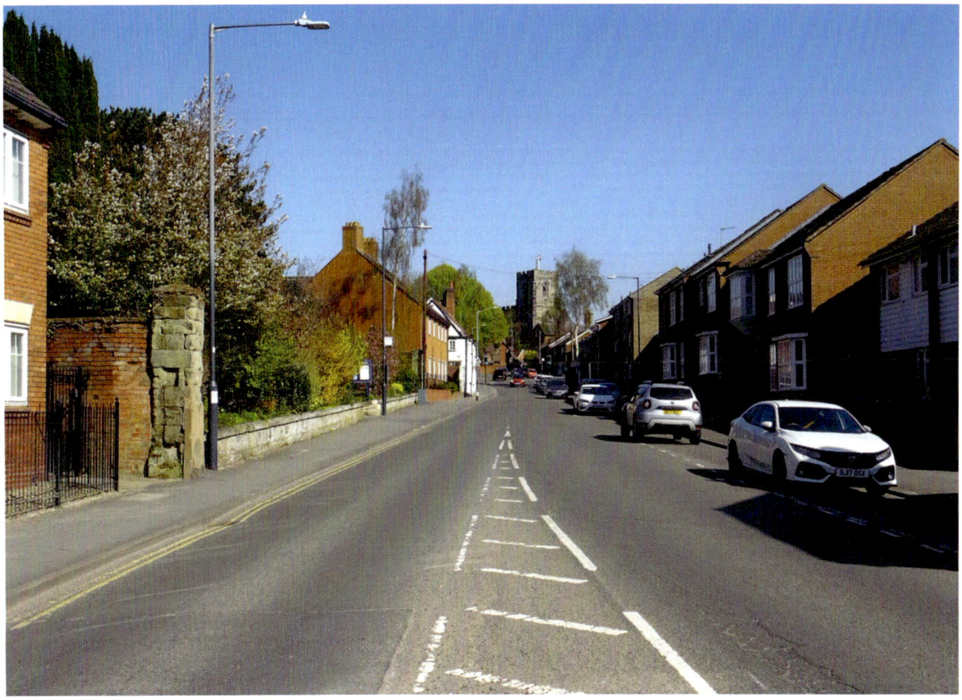

Friar Street. A thirteenth-century Dominican Friary was once located here opposite St Paul's Church; it was demolished in the sixteenth century. Excavations in 1972 found pieces of stained glass and human bones which are now held by Warwick Museum.

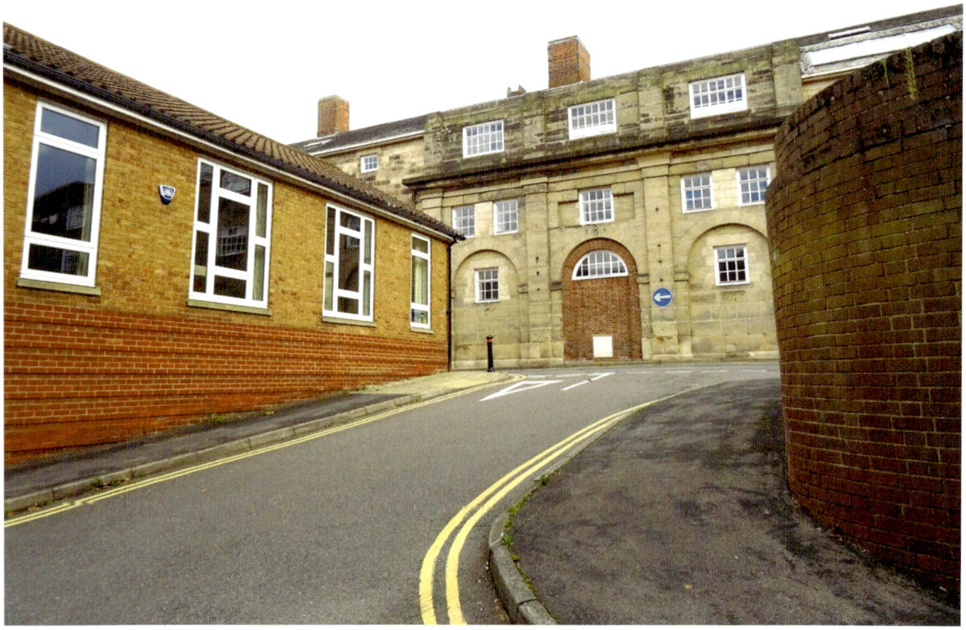

Excavations carried out on this site, between Joyce Pool (now demolished) and Barrack Street in 1972, revealed traces of the eleventh-century town ditch and fourteenth-century town wall.

the town wall adjoin the north side of the two gates, but the approximate position of the rest is suggested by the layout of the streets which encircle the town.

The streets outside the line of the wall and ditch are now called Bowling Green Street, Theatre Street, Joyce Pool (demolished), Chapel Street, Gerrard Street and Mill Street. Those inside the line of the wall are Market Street, Barrack Street and The Butts but may have also included Brittain Lane and Back Hills. However, excavations carried out in 1972 between Joyce Pool and Barrack Street in advance of redevelopment revealed substantial traces of the northern defences of the town. These included a 'robber' trench on the line of the fourteenth-century town wall and the eleventh-century defensive ditch with a timber palisade. The ditch was recorded as being 25 feet wide and 9 feet deep in places and cut deep into the sandstone.

Outside Northgate the suburb was centred on the Saltisford, by way of which ran a salt-way from Droitwich to Warwick. Here was situated St Michael's Church and Leper Hospital founded in the latter twelfth and thirteenth centuries, and St Sepulchre's Priory founded in 1109 which was located close to Northgate. The Saltisford suburb stretched along Birmingham Road as far as the ford through Goysel or Goose Brook.

The Church of St Michael was founded by Roger, Earl of Warwick in 1135, becoming the chapel of the Leper Hospital later. To accommodate the scourge of leprosy, the Leper Hospital was situated on the outskirts of the town on a main thoroughfare, as were other such hospitals throughout the country, and was first referenced in 1275. Its use

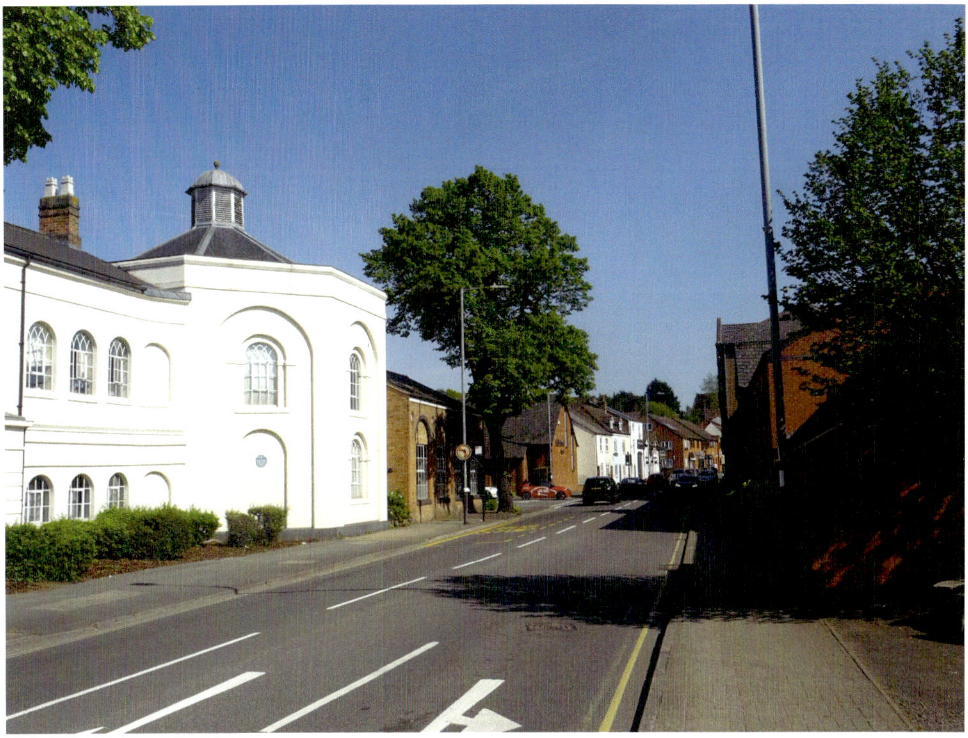

The Saltisford – part of the old saltway from Droitwich to Warwick. The gasworks were built in 1822 and were one of the first in the world. It closed in 1953.

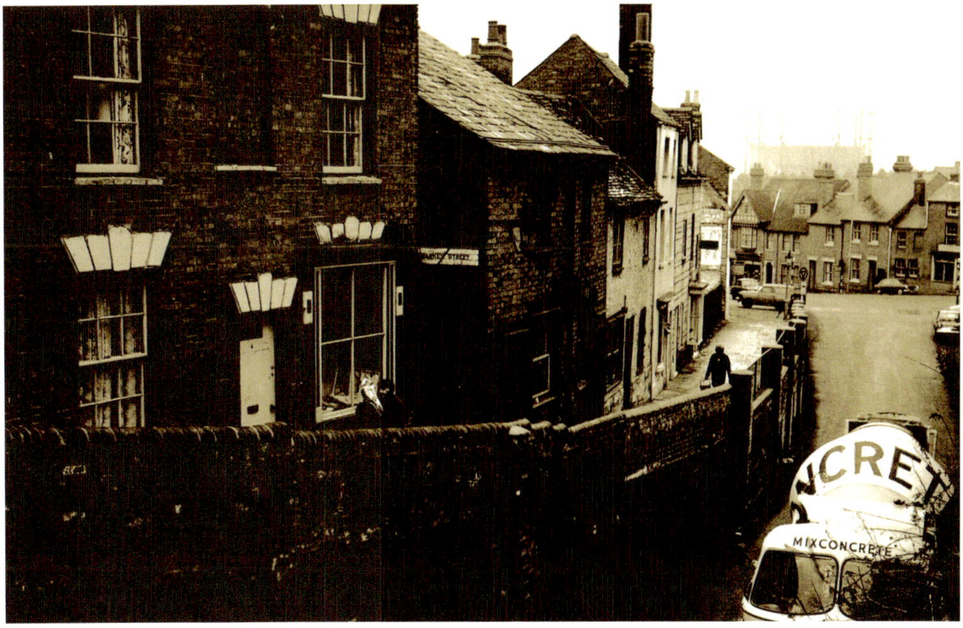

The Holloway leading to Saltisford. In the background is one of the three original gasholders which have long since been demolished. (Image author's collection)

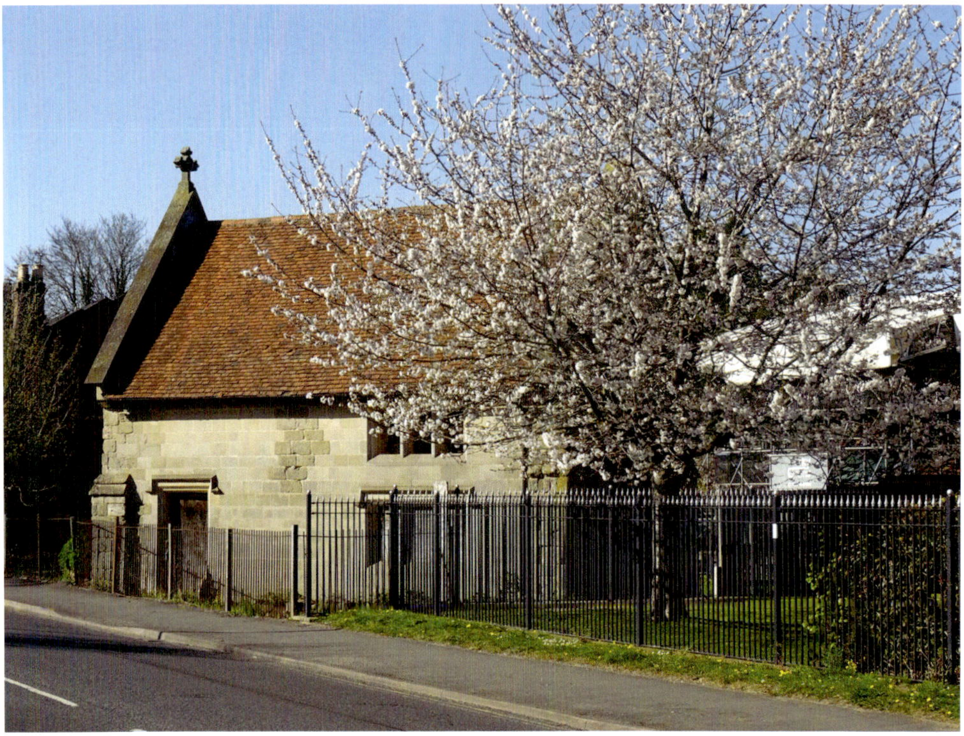

St Michael's medieval church, founded by Roger, Earl of Warwick in 1135, later to become the chapel of the Leper Hospital.

as a leper hospital had probably declined as the disease died out and was then used as a hospital for the poor. By 1540 the hospital was said to be 'much in ruin' and by 1545 it was leased to layman Richard Fisher, who distributed alms to the poor and gave lodging to four poor men. The last priest recorded acquired office in 1557. The chapel and Master's House were converted into cottages in the seventeenth/eighteenth centuries.

An archaeological excavation carried out in December 2004 on the site of the medieval Leper Hospital, a Scheduled Ancient Monument, revealed the remains of stone wall foundations, a pebble yard surface, postholes and pits in the area between the chapel and Master's House. It also recorded the earliest evidence for human activity in the area and signs of Roman occupation with the discovery of a Roman coin.

Eastgate was one of the three main gates which allowed access into the town. It was reconstructed in the early fifteenth century when the chapel of St Peter was built above it. This double-arched edifice has a wide arch spanning the original roadway and a smaller arch for pedestrians. The gate was altered and re-faced in the later eighteenth century, and it was probably at this time that the roadway diversion to the south was constructed. St Peter's Chapel was rebuilt in Gothic style by Francis Hiron in 1786 which was most likely when the crenellations and pinnacles were added. The chapel was used as a schoolroom in the sixteenth and nineteenth centuries, notably by the King's Grammar School, and Bablake, a Charity School. More recently it was used as a schoolroom for the King's High School for Girls.

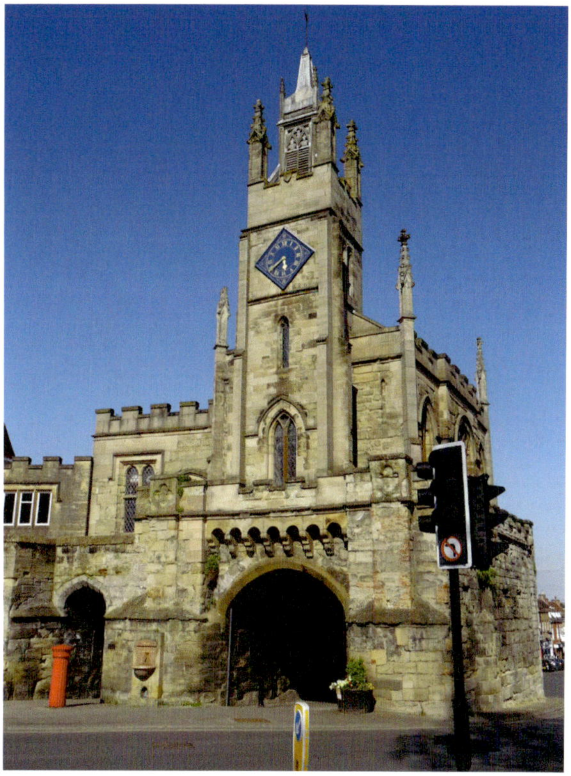

Right: Eastgate, a double-arched construction with St Peter's Chapel above, is one of the two remaining gates in Warwick and is adjoined by part of the fourteenth-century town wall, as seen by John Leland, sixteenth-century traveller.

Below: Eastgate – a Grade II Scheduled Ancient Monument built *c.* 1420, now in private ownership. This aspect is the most likely site for displaying the remains of John Sugar, hanged, drawn and quartered in 1604.

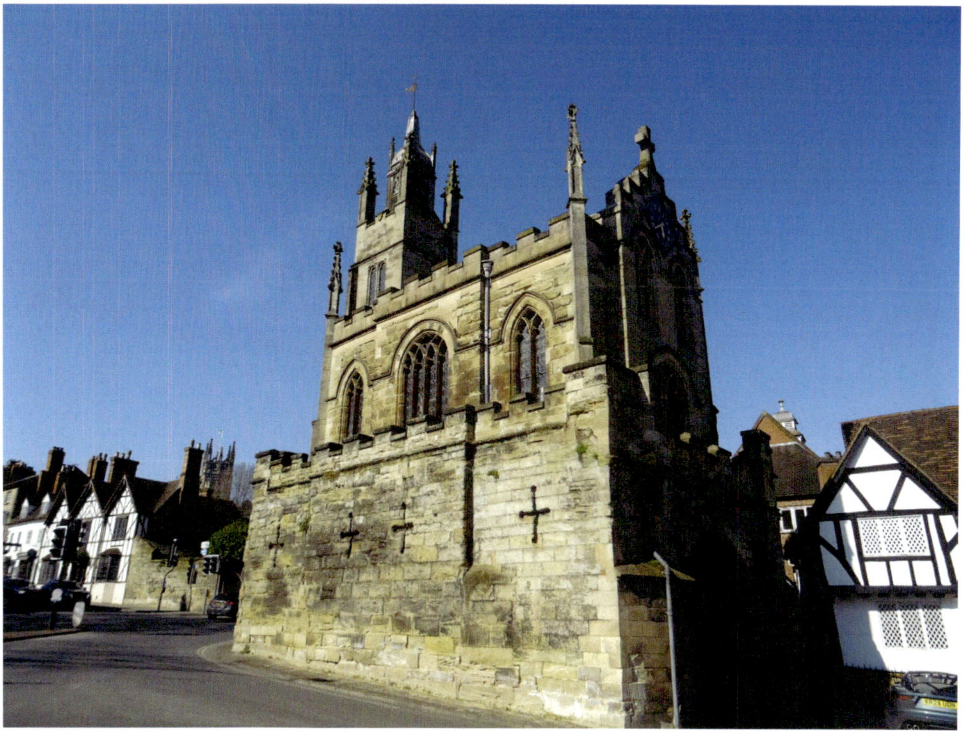

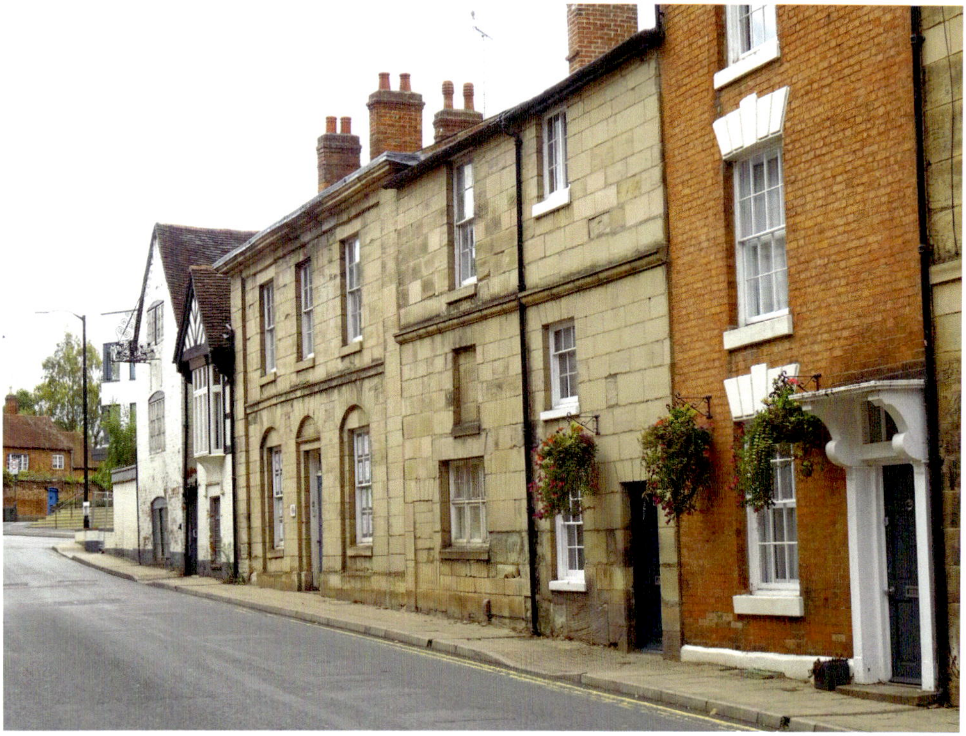

The Butts. The name was probably derived from when men practised archery with a longbow, which was mandatory in Tudor times and *the* weapon of choice.

Eastgate may also have served a more sinister purpose. Catholic priest John Sugar and his assistant Robert Grissold had been held in Warwick gaol for a year as Catholic recusant priests. They were executed at Gallows Hill in 1604. John Sugar was hanged, drawn and quartered and Charles Lines, in *The Book of Warwick*, says his remains were displayed on one of the gates. This was most likely to have been Eastgate, however no reference has been found to it.

The eastern suburb comprised of Smith Street leading on to Coten End, together with St Nicholas Church Street, Mill Street, Gaol Hall Lane, Poke Lane and Dog Lane. Located here were St Nicholas' Church, the county gaol and St John's Hospital. South of the River Avon was the suburb of Bridge End where Mill Street, Cross Street and Warytree Street met. Close by was the house of the Templars and the Templars watermill.

With their origins in France, the Knights Templar were a Catholic medieval military order and an important elite element of the Crusades armies. They were given a manor beyond the bridge on the south side of Warwick by Roger, Earl of Warwick in the twelfth century. The moated manor was transferred to the Knights Hospitallers in 1324. After the Dissolution of the Hospitallers in 1540 the manor was reunited with the castle estates in 1549 but was known to have gone by 1786.

Several of these street names have now disappeared, being Gaol Hall Lane, Poke Lane, Dog Lane and Warytree Street. Warytree Street was changed to Gallows Street in 1823 and led to the gallows on Gallows Hill, a stretch of which is now Banbury Road.

The historic main streets formed a cross and tie between the gates on which many of the principal houses in the town were situated. These were High Street (High Pavement) and Jury Street, intersected by Castle Street, Church Street and Northgate Street and were described by Leland as 'the beauty and glory of the town'.

One house of note in High Street is Alderson House. Frank Collier, Archivist for Alderson House, records that it had its origins in the mid-fourteenth century when Thomas Beauchamp, Earl of Warwick acquired the existing property from John le Boteller. It was burnt down in the Great Fire of 1694 and rebuilt by 1696. This grand house, now listed as a Grade II building, was purchased in 1961 by Alderson House (Warwick) Limited on behalf of several Masonic Lodges based in Warwick. It was named after Gerald Alderson, a prominent Warwickshire Freemason and benefactor.

The most significant of Warwick's defences was the castle to the south. This formidable structure was referred to by Sir William Dugdale, the seventeenth-century antiquary, as 'the most princely seat within these Midland parts of the realm'. Its strategic position, being close to the centre of England, was of considerable military importance during the Middle Ages, which saw the castle as more significant than the town. Its earls played their parts as loyal subjects of the Crown, being a bastion against rebellion. Murder, intrigue, scandal, conspiracy and mayhem are all part of the rich tapestry of the colourful history of Warwick Castle.

The title Earl of Warwick was to descend from the de Beaumonts to William Mauduit and eventually to the Beauchamp family. A staunch supporter of Henry III,

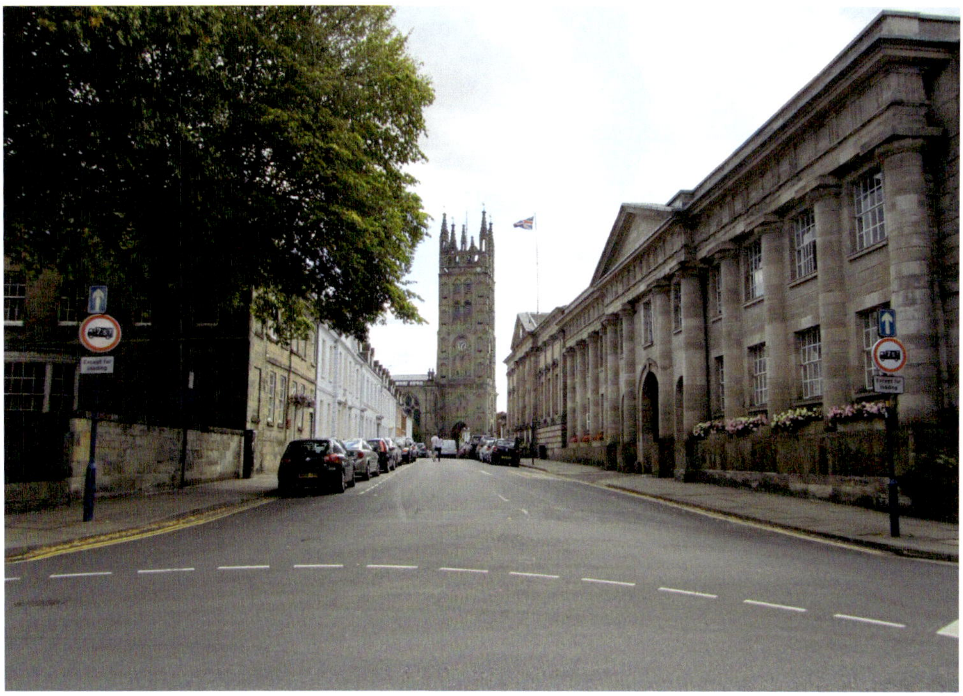

Northgate Street, described as 'the most handsome Georgian street in the Midlands' by Alec Clifton-Taylor in *Six More English Towns*.

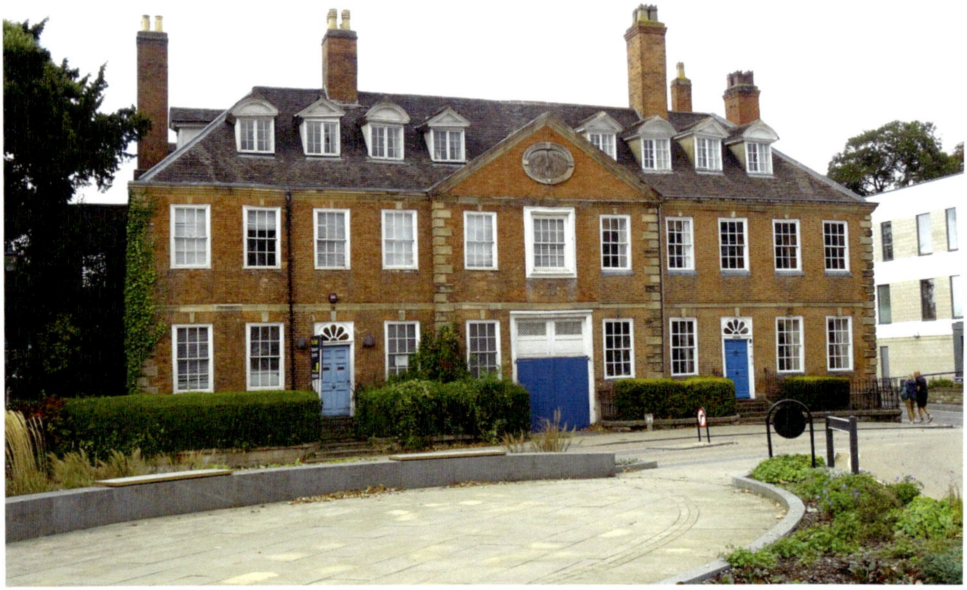

Northgate House is a Grade II listed building believed to have been constructed in the late seventeenth century. This replaced the inn and cottages that had previously stood on the site and which were destroyed in the fire of 1694.

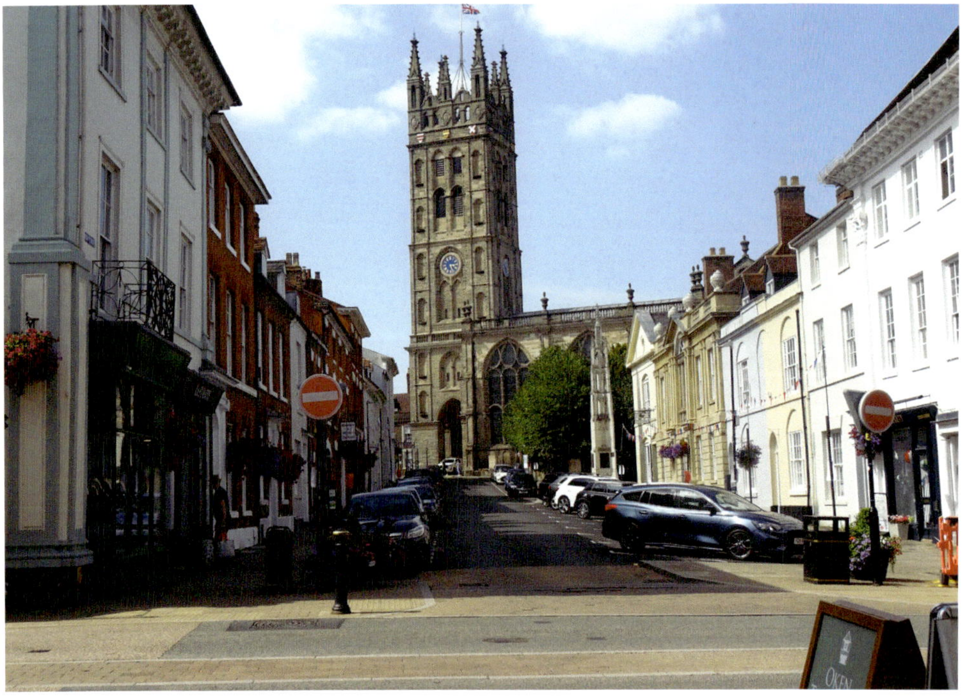

Church Street/Castle Street intersects with High Street/Jury Street forming a cross on the same street pattern, as shown in the 'Ground Plott of Warwick' by Hollar *c.* 1630.

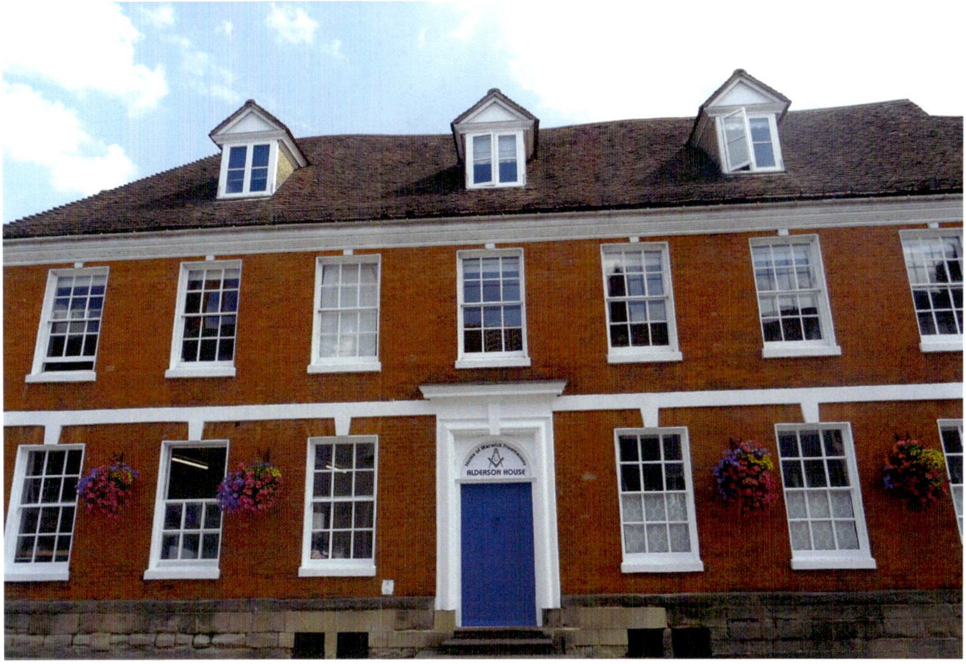

Alderson House is a Grade II listed building named after Gerald Alderson, a prominent Mason and benefactor.

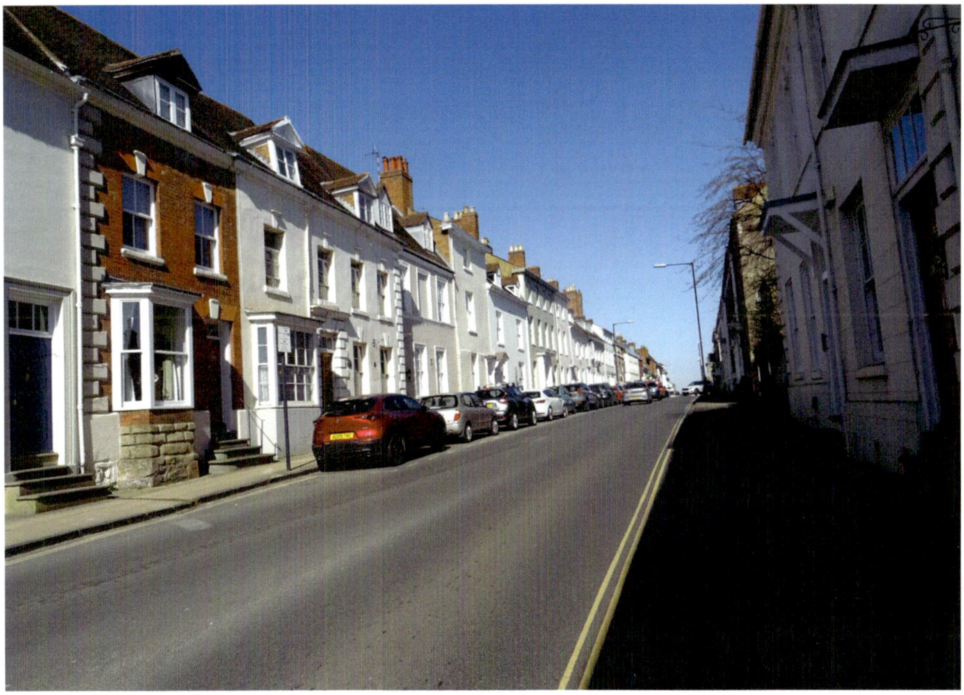

High Street. These houses were built in the style of William and Mary in 1695 to attract the professional classes to settle in Warwick and are still aesthetically pleasing today.

William Mauduit was a participant in the Second Barons' War in 1264–67. During this time Warwick Castle was captured by John Giffard who held Kenilworth Castle in 1264 for Simon de Montfort. William Mauduit and his wife were taken prisoner and held at Kenilworth Castle until a ransom of 1,900 marks was paid. John Rous, fifteenth-century chronicler, says that 'the walls along the north eastern side of the castle were destroyed so that it should be no strength to the King'.

Successive Beauchamps included Guy de Beauchamp, also known as the 'Black Hound of Arden' as dubbed by Piers Gaveston, Duke of Cornwall and favourite of Edward II. The scurrilous nickname referred to the earl's swarthy appearance. Gaveston was to meet a very untimely end at the hands of this particular earl, who swore he would feel the 'Black Hound's bite'. The haughty Gaveston, much disliked by the barons, was exiled by the king but returned to England. Captured at Deddington by Guy de Beauchamp, Piers Gaveston was brought under guard to Warwick, tried at the castle and taken to Gaveswich (now Blacklow Hill) where he was summarily beheaded in 1312. A cross and plaque erected in 1821 by Bertie Greatheed of nearby Guys Cliffe Mansion stands on Blacklow Hill, marking the spot of the execution of Gaveston.

Guy's Cliffe overlooking the River Avon was the site of the chapel of St Dubritius, founded as an oratory by Dubritius, Bishop of Warwick, *c.* AD 600 and dedicated to Mary Magdalene. Below the chapel on a rocky outcrop is a cave where the legendary Saxon nobleman Guy of Warwick is said to have spent his life as a hermit after returning from

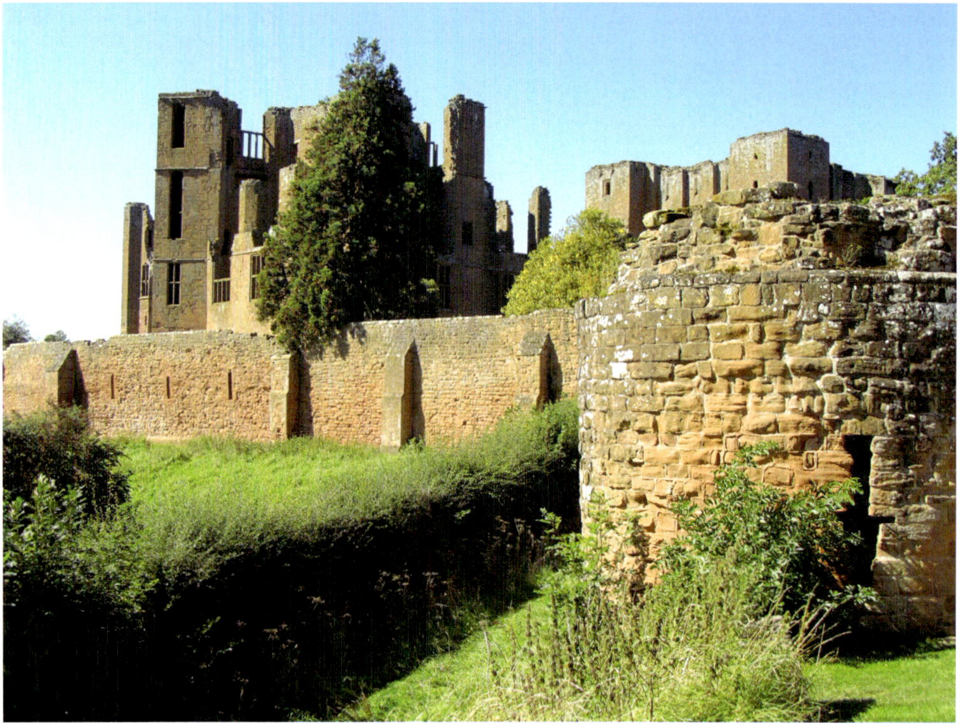

Ruins of Kenilworth Castle. Earl William Maudit and wife Katherine were captured, taken to the castle and held for ransom by Simon de Montfort during the Second Barons' War in 1264–67.

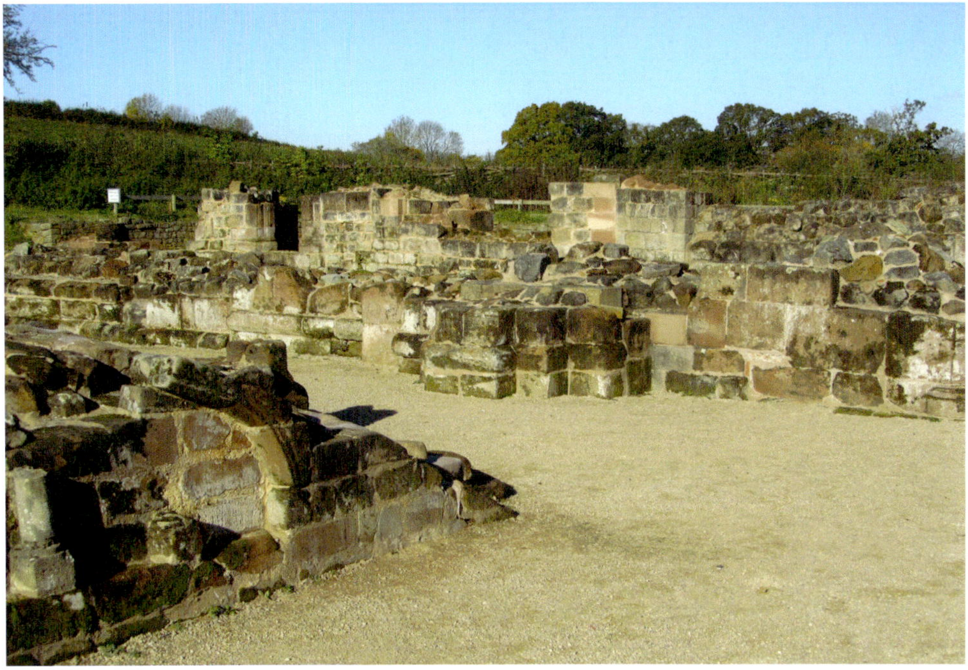

Above: The ruins of Bordesley Abbey, Worcestershire. This was the burial place of Guy de Beauchamp, 'Black Hound of Arden', on his death in 1315. A casualty of Henry VIII's Dissolution of the Monasteries in 1538, the site is now an excavation project.

Right: Erected by Bertie Greatheed of Guy's Cliffe Manor in 1821, this monument stands in the hollow of a rock on Blacklow Hill where the execution of Piers Gaveston, favourite of Edward II, took place in 1312.

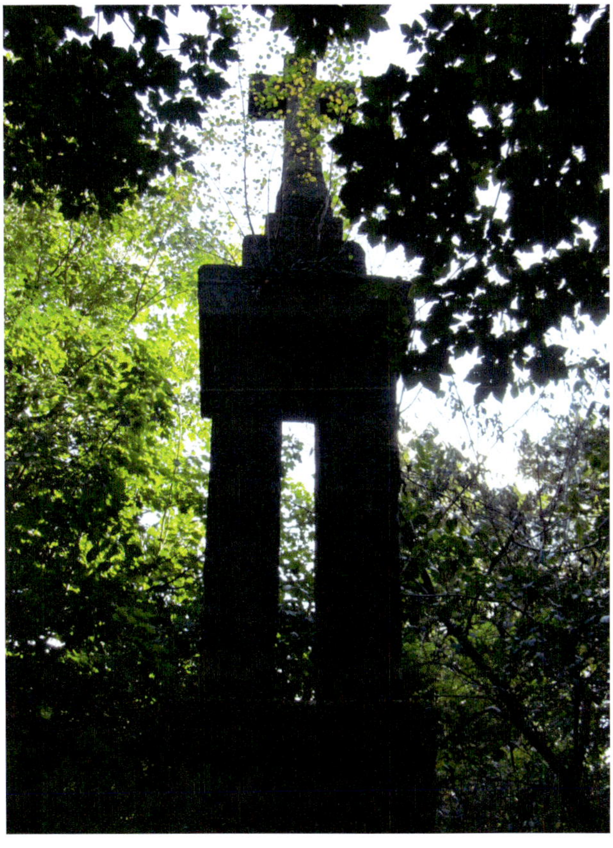

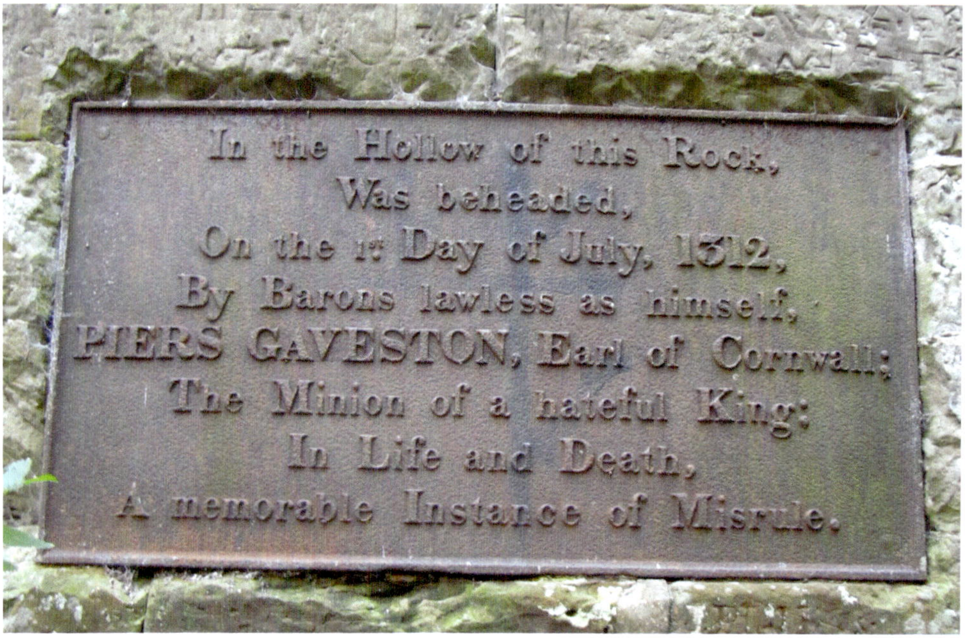

A plaque at the foot of the monument is inscribed: *In the hollow of this rock was beheaded on the 17 day of July 1312 by barons lawless as himself, Piers Gaveston, Earl of Cornwall, the minion of a hateful King in life and death, a memorable instance of misrule.*

his pilgrimage in the Holy Lands. Guy slaughtered the notorious Dun Cow who terrorised the villagers in Dunsmore Heath and also Colbrand, the fearsome Danish warrior who terrorised Winchester. After marrying Lady Felice, daughter of Rohund, Earl of Warwick, Guy left to fight in the Crusades. On his return and sickened by the killing, Guy retired to live in a cave at Guy's Cliffe until his death.

John Rous, fifteenth-century antiquary, retired to the hermitage at Guy's Cliffe in the later stage of his life in 1432 and became one of the two chantry priests.

The Earls of Warwick were to wield much influence not only in Warwick but also in the country and beyond in France. They played a crucial role in the Hundred Years' War with France with their military leadership. A decisive victory at the Battle of Crecy in 1346 was secured by Thomas, son of Guy de Beauchamp, and he was also credited with capturing the Archbishop of Sens at the Battle of Poitiers. It was the enormous ransom he secured for the archbishop which partially paid for the construction of Poitiers Tower (Caesar's Tower). His son, Thomas, succeeded to the title on his death in 1369.

Successive earl Richard Beauchamp, described as a chivalrous knight, also fought in the Hundred Years' War with Henry V. His leadership and strategic decisions were crucial in shaping the course of the war and future of England. He was responsible for bringing Joan of Arc to trial and overseeing her execution at Rouen in 1431. Richard Beauchamp gave instructions in his will for a chapel to be built on the south side of St Mary's Collegiate Church and he was subsequently interred there on his death in 1439.

During the Middle Ages the earls held complete control of the town. From feudal lords honing their skills in battle to town civic influencers and benefactors, the earls have played

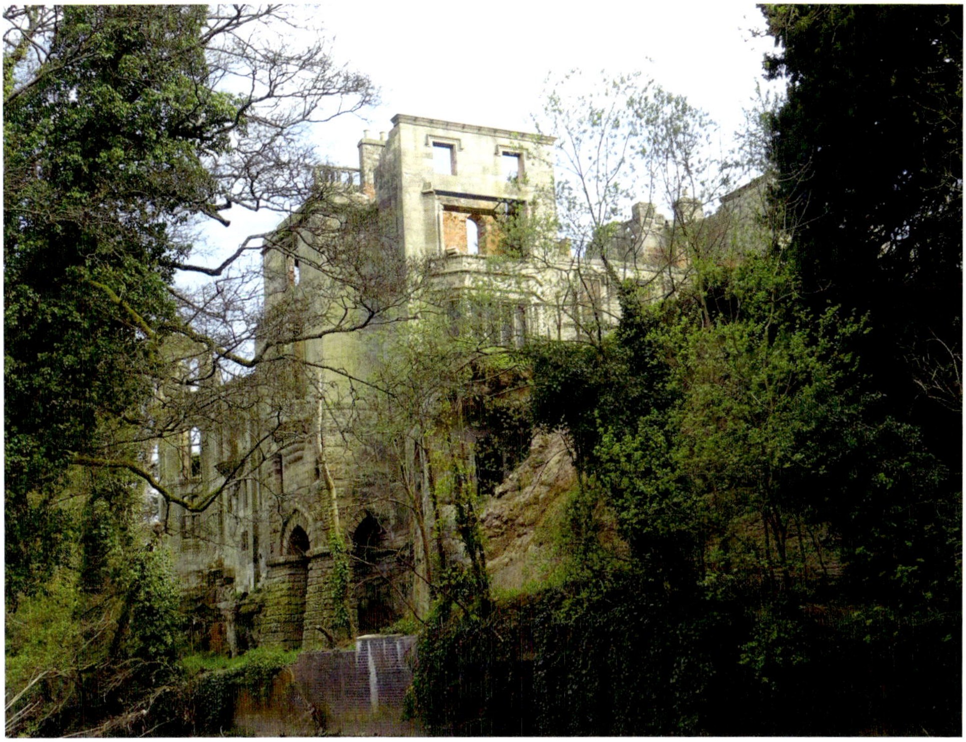

The ruins of Guy's Cliffe, home to Bertie Greatheed and later the Heber-Percys. Beneath the rocky outcrop is a cave where the Saxon nobleman Guy of Warwick lived as a hermit until his death after returning from the Crusades.

a significant part in the history of Warwick. Most significant of all: step forward Richard Neville, 'Warwick the Kingmaker' and Captain of Calais. Richard Neville inherited the title and estates in 1450 through marriage to Anne Beauchamp, sister of Henry Beauchamp, first Duke of Warwick, a member of a wealthy, dominant and influential dynasty. He was to become very influential in shaping the monarchy during the Wars of the Roses.

A powerful, wealthy and charismatic feudal lord, Richard Neville was to become a turncoat during battles of the Wars of the Roses, switching his allegiance from Lancastrian Henry VI to Yorkist Edward, Earl of March. He proclaimed Edward as king in 1461 after the Battle of Towton and defeat of Henry VI. However, Richard Neville and Edward IV were to fall out following Edward's secret marriage to Elizabeth Woodville and his signing a treaty with Burgundy, which undermined Neville's own political ambitions in making a French alliance by marrying Edward to the sister-in-law of Louis XI. Neville subsequently captured Edward following a rebellion in 1469 and held him prisoner at the castle and attempted to rule in his name. Following protests by the people and Parliament, Neville was forced to release Edward.

Upon Neville's death at the Battle of Barnet in 1471, where he once again fought on the side of the Lancastrians, the castle and estates passed to George Plantagenet, Duke of Clarence and later his son, Edward Plantagenet. It is said that George Plantagenet was drowned in a butt of malmsey. Edward Plantagenet was executed for treason. He was the seventh and last Plantagenet Earl. On his death in 1479 the castle and estates reverted to the Crown. Neville's daughter, Ann, was later to become Queen on her marriage to Richard III.

After a considerable lapse in time, John Dudley was newly created Earl of Warwick in 1547. He too was to perish on the scaffold for his part in the plot to place Lady Jane Grey on the throne after the death of Edward VI. John Dudley had also plotted to secure his fortunes through the marriage of his son Guildford to Lady Jane Grey. These were executed on 12 February 1554 in the Tower of London. Although the whole of the Dudley family was attainted and sons Ambrose, Robert and Henry were also imprisoned in the Tower of London, they were later released and pardoned and the estates were restored to Ambrose, who regained the title in 1561 for his services to Elizabeth I.

One of the greatest events in the history of Warwick was the visit of Elizabeth I. While occupying the castle, Ambrose Dudley was bestowed the doubtful honour of being visited by the Queen. The honour was doubtful because although conferring great prestige, it proved to be a very costly affair for anyone obliged to accommodate the royal party. During her Progress the Queen visited the great houses either as a favour or, if she was displeased with the incumbent, as a means of bankrupting them by overstaying her welcome. Elizabeth travelled with over 400 carts carrying her baggage and was accompanied by many courtiers and servants, all of whom had to be fed and accommodated.

Peering through the mists of time, we are given a glimpse of Elizabethan splendour. Sixteenth-century Warwick Town Clerk and Bailiff John Fisher gives a fulsome description of Elizabeth's visit to the castle which brings to life the pageantry of the Queen's progress through the town. When the Queen entered Warwick, she was accompanied by Lady Warwick who was bestowed the great honour of riding in Elizabeth's coach. In attendance were Lord Burghley (Treasurer), Earl of Sussex (Lord Chamberlain), Lord Howard of Effingham (Lord Privy Seal), Earl of Rutland, Earl of Huntingly, Earl of Leicester (Master of the Horses), together with many other bishops, lords and ladies.

Bailiff Robert Philips greeted the Queen by making a long speech, on the conclusion of which he approached her carriage and on bended knee, offered her majesty a purse containing twenty sovereigns. Elizabeth graciously accepted the offering and the whole cavalcade then rode in order two by two before her majesty from Ford Mill (Tach Brook) until they came to the castle gate. Here they were marshalled by the heralds and gentlemen ushers clothed in coats of 'puke' (a dark colour between black and russet) laid over with lace. The principal burgesses were clothed in gowns of 'puke' lined with satin and damask. The bailiff, sumptuously dressed in a gown of scarlet, was placed before the Queen and on the right-hand of Lord Compton, High Sheriff of Warwickshire.

Elizabeth visited Warwick Castle twice. The first occasion was a brief interlude during a summer progress in 1566. On the second visit in 1572 she lodged in the castle for four nights between 11 and 18 August while on a visit to Kenilworth Castle, seat of Robert Dudley. As the castle at that time was in a considerable state of decay, a timber building was erected for her accommodation. The custodian of the castle, Ambrose Dudley, had to vacate the premises to the nearby Priory in order that Elizabeth and her retinue could be accommodated.

To ensure the Queen was well entertained, Dudley provided lavishly for her amusement with a mock battle in the Temple Field below the castle walls and culminating in a splendid firework display. Elizabethan recorder John Fisher states that the firework display went badly awry when a fireball hit a house on the bridge of an elderly couple asleep in their premises and set it alight. They were rescued amid much hullabaloo, but the house was burned down. Next day at her command the couple were brought before the Queen who compensated them with the sum of £25.

Among the onlookers of the splendour as Elizabeth and her retinue made their way to the castle were the poor and needy whose lowly status had been assigned at birth. Social mobility, although possible, was virtually non-existent for the poor and their station in life as ordained would continue. They struggled to survive and those able to work laboured usually on the land from sunrise to sunset during the winter and from sunrise to early evening in the summer, their only break being Sunday and major religious festivals.

The poor labouring on the land were further disadvantaged when the arable land was left to fallow or become pasture which led to displacement. In 1517 the Priory of St Sepulchre was reported to have converted 80 acres of arable land to pasture which deprived eleven persons of work.

In 1571, John Fisher, recorder of *The Black Book of Warwick*, complained that 'the number of poor was very great and that they were relieved only by the charitable devotion of the inhabitants with collections in the church'. A survey made in 1586 on the insistence of the Puritan master of The Lord Leycester Hospital, Thomas Cartwright, 'touching on the disorder of beggars' described 114 adults and 113 children in St Mary's parish as poor, of whom fifty adults and sixty children were beggars. Seven adults and a child were declared to be able-bodied, and one adult was ordered to be whipped and find himself a master. Eight families including at least as many children were to be sent from the town to their places of origin, mostly in the county but one as far afield as Wales.

The plague in the winter of 1604 strained the resources of the overseers. An attempt was made to decrease the number of people chargeable on the rates by removing inmates and lodgers from the town. By 1628 all inmates were required to give pledges on entering the town for fear they would become a burden on the rates. Charitable institutions in Warwick included St Michael's medieval church and hospital in the Saltisford and Thomas Oken and Nicholas Eyffler's alms-houses built in the sixteenth and seventeenth centuries on the Back Hills (Castle Hill).

Ambrose Dudley's premature death was brought about by a war wound that turned gangrenous resulting in the amputation of his leg from which he died a few days later. Following the death of Ambrose Dudley in 1590, who died without an heir, the castle once again reverted to the Crown, during which years it fell into a state of considerable decay.

Despite the castle being in a considerable state of decay, a very large stable built outside the castle gate by Richard Beauchamp in 1423 was still standing in 1605 which proved fortuitous for the Gunpowder Plot conspirators. They stole horses from the stable on which to make their escape following their meeting at a pub in Dunchurch where they learned that the gunpowder plot had failed. Their bid to escape was thwarted and in the event, they were soon captured.

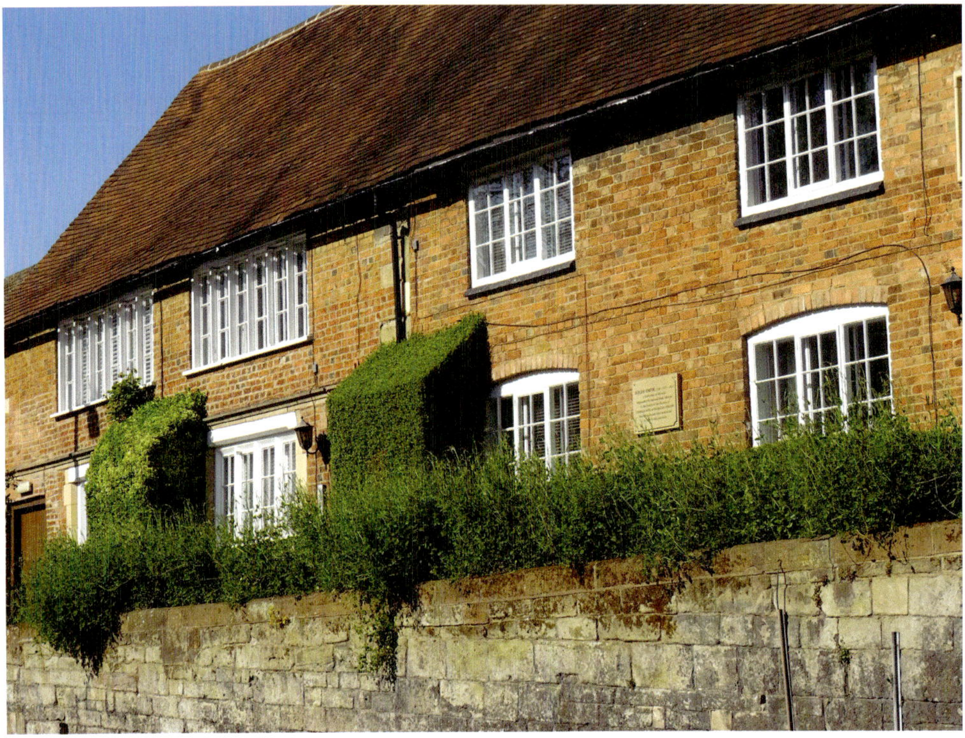

Almshouses on Castle Hill, administered by the charities of Thomas Oken and Nicholas Eyffler, town benefactors, founded in the sixteenth and seventeenth centuries.

It was in this ruinous state that the castle was bestowed on Sir Fulke Greville by James I in 1604. Sir Fulke Greville was a Recorder in 1610 and possessed a significant number of properties in the town. He was created 1st Baron Lord Brooke of Beauchamps Court in 1621. Undaunted by the magnitude of the task ahead, Fulke Greville began the restoration of the castle and converted it into a fine country house which was very much in vogue at that time. His murder in 1628 by his manservant, Ralph Hayward, gave rise to the present-day attraction of the 'Ghost Tower' where it is said he haunts his former study.

Another Fulke Greville, third son of Robert Greville who was killed at Lichfield, was elected to Parliament and credited with helping the people of Warwick who had lost their homes and possessions in the Great Fire of 1694. On 4 November 1695, William III was entertained at the castle. A spectacular show of illuminations was created with pitch and tar devised by Nicholas Paris and burnt on Guy's Tower. The townsfolk were also included in the celebrations and provided with 100 gallons of punch from Guy's Pot.

The title Earl of Warwick was bestowed on Robert Lord Rich in 1618 and continued with that family until 1759 when the last member, Edward Rich, died without a male heir. The Richs' were descendants of Richard Rich who brought about the downfall and execution of Sir Thomas More in 1535. The title was then restored to the Grevilles together with John Dudley's famous emblem, the bear and ragged staff, and has descended through that family until the present day.

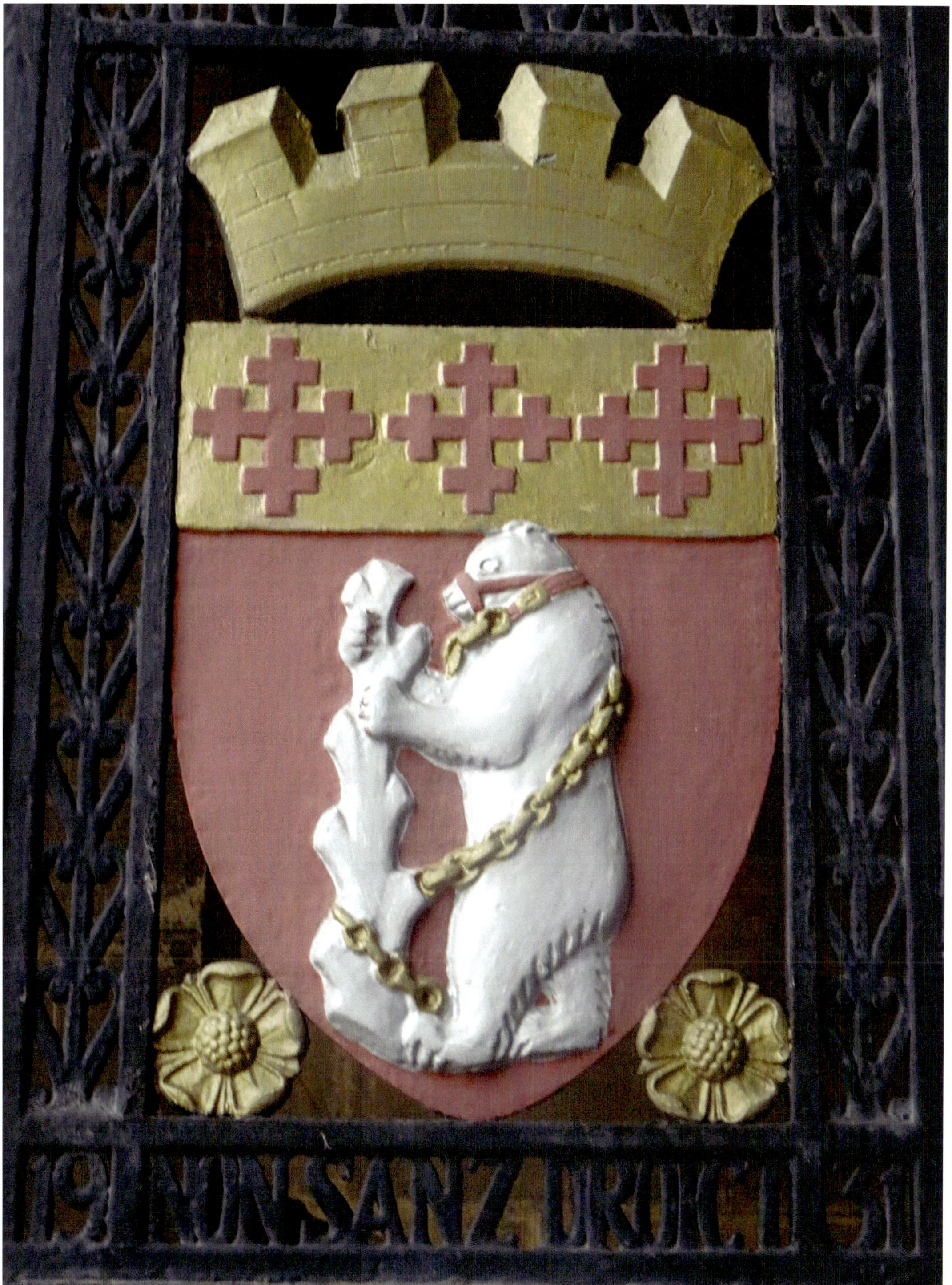

The Bear and Ragged Staff with the motto *Non Sans Droict* – Not Without Right. This was the emblem of John Dudley, Earl of Warwick.

It was perhaps in the latter part of the sixteenth century that Warwick reached the peak of its medieval prosperity. By the reign of Elizabeth I, the population was approaching 3,000, due to rising birth rates and falling death rates. The visit of the Queen would have generated considerable trade. *The Book of Warwick* states that Mr Styles records that in a list made between 1571 and 1575 there were six companies of tradesmen: walkers (fullers) and dyers; printmakers; glovers and skinners; grocers, fishmongers, butchers, bakers; drapers, tailors, mercers; and haberdashers. Butchers were located mostly in High Pavement and Jury Street, mercers, grocers and haberdashers in High Pavement, Church Street and Castle Street, while tanners, who were numerous, were in West Street, Saltisford, Smith Street and Bridge End.

By 1684 the number of companies had increased to twelve and included shoemakers, saddlers, masons and tilers, carpenters and joiners, flax dressers, silk and woollen weavers and smiths. Smiths were the most numerous of the freemen among the companies and this was the only trade for which Warwick had a widespread reputation. Smith Street beyond Eastgate takes its name from the medieval smiths and armourers. The Smith Street suburb reached as far as St John's Brook which flowed from Wedgnock Park and fed the fishponds of St Sepulchre's Priory on its way to the River Avon.

The trade companies were an important feature of the urban economy and replaced the medieval craft guilds through which corporations exercised economic control. In Warwick they seem to have owed their existence to corporation initiative but were supervised in many of their activities by the Court Leet.

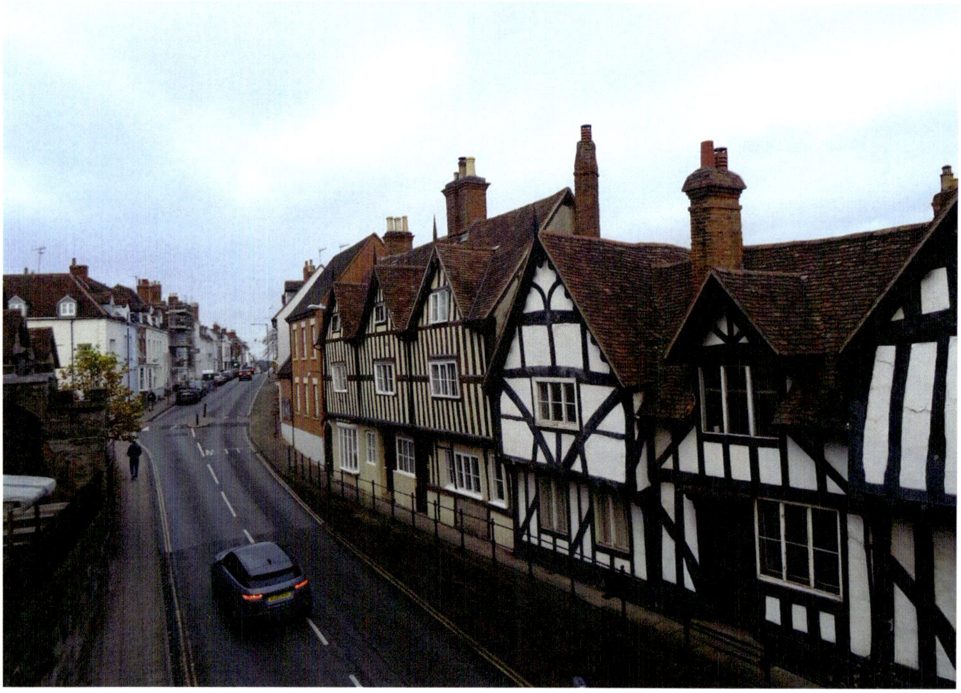

High Street (High Pavement). Situated on this street was the Friends Meeting House, a Quaker house. The Great Fire of 1694 started in this region.

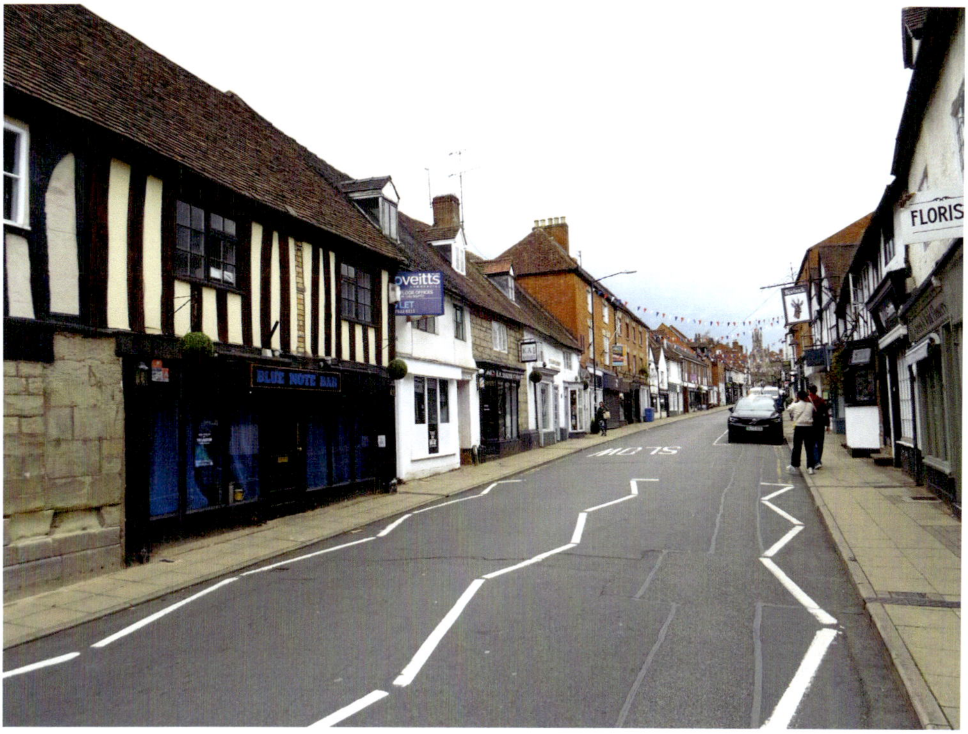

Smith Street was once the abode of the gunsmiths, goldsmiths, armourers and the Jewish quarter.

The Court Leet was established by Royal Charter in 1554. This gave the Earl of Warwick authority to ensure good practice in trade. For example, the Leet as early as 1549–50 had ordered that a baker should not sell his wares outside the borough. The Court Leet also appointed bread weighers, flesh tasters and ale tasters. The earl also had the authority to try by jury and punish all crimes committed within his jurisdiction except for the most serious crimes which were committed to the Court of King's Bench. Apart from the company headed by mercers, the corporation was able to control membership. This was a power which could be exercised for political and social as well as economic reasons.

Trade was restricted mostly to serving the needs of the castle; however, one product of the town in the seventeenth century was of wider appeal. Nicholas Paris, described as a gunsmith in 1684, enjoyed a reputation as an ironworker whose works extended far afield. He was also employed at the castle between 1677 and 1713 supplying metal fittings for the castle fire engine and mill and was responsible for regilding the effigy of Richard Beauchamp at St Mary's Church. His brother, Samuel, was regularly employed mending and maintaining clocks at the castle between 1682 and 1715.

During the turbulent years of the Civil War which started in October 1642 with the first major battle at Edgehill, the castle was fortunate to be held by the Parliamentarians (Roundheads) which meant it escaped the fate of other castles which saw them bombarded with cannon throughout the Protectorate of Oliver Cromwell. In preparation at the outset of the Civil War custodian of the castle Robert Greville, Lord Brooke strengthened its defences between January and May 1642. The castle was later attacked and besieged by a

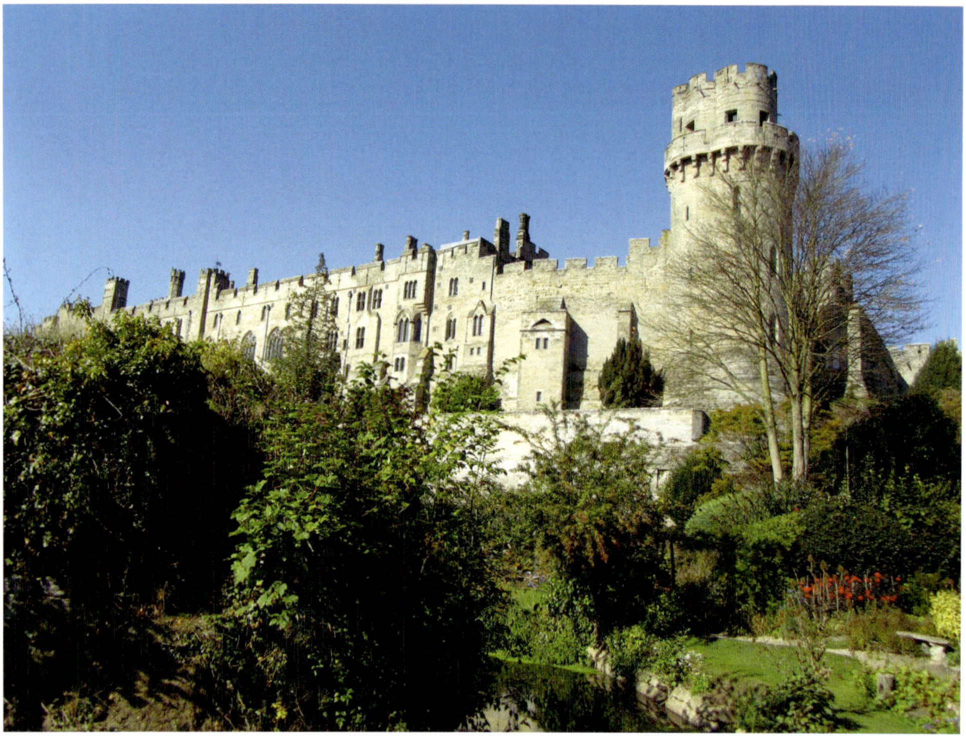

The castle was ably held by Parliamentarians during the siege of 1642 in the Civil War. Guy's and Caesar's Towers were constructed in the fourteenth century and held prisoners from the Civil War.

Royalist (Cavaliers) army under the command of the Earl of Northampton. The castle was ably held by a Parliamentarian garrison commanded by Sir Edward Peyto of Chesterton in the absence of Lord Brooke.

The disastrous effects of the war were experienced in the town. An extract from a letter written by a gentleman in Warwick to a friend in London reads:

> There came letters to the houses, informing the true state of things at Warwick Castle; that Sir Edward Peyto very valiantly keeps the same, notwithstanding the often attempts against him by the Earle of Northampton and his Company, who have possessed themselves of Warwick Towne and do daily commit great spoile and outrage against any that seem well affected to the Parliament.

The attack was carried out by hauling the cannon to the top of nearby St Mary's Church and firing shots at the castle. These barely made an impression on the castle but did kill several people in the town. The earl was forced to abandon his plans to capture it and withdrew when Parliamentarian reinforcements under the command of the Earl of Essex who had been fighting a few miles away at Edgehill were known to be approaching the castle. Townsfolk would have watched as prisoners taken at the Battle of Edgehill in 1642 were brought to the castle to be confined in Caesar's and Guy's Towers. Maimed soldiers were cared for in the Vineyard House.

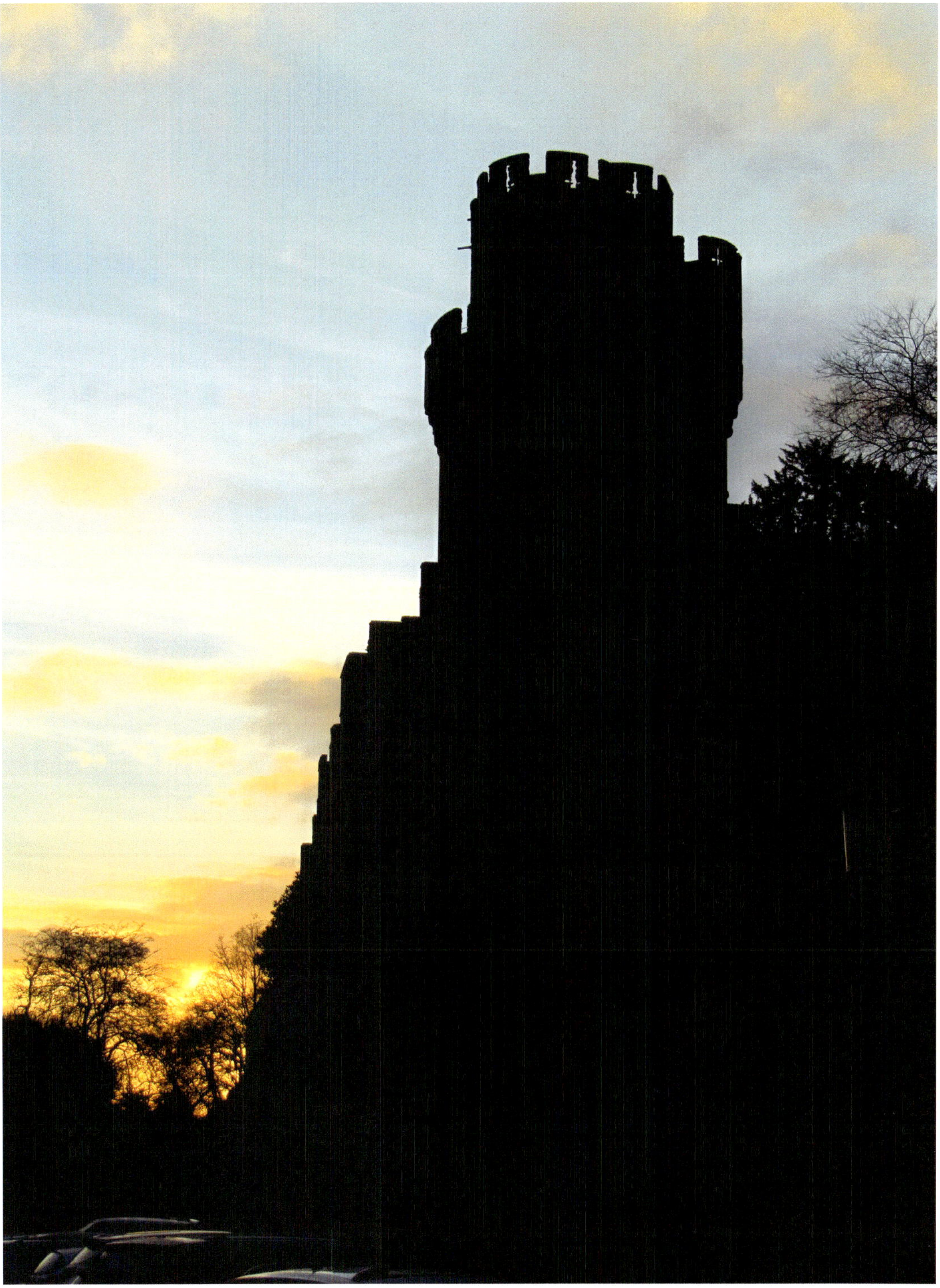

The formidable Caesar's Tower. A dungeon in the base of Caesar's Tower was probably used concurrently with the gaol during 1497–1507 when the castle was in the hands of the Crown.

Robert Greville, Lord Brooke, a stalwart Parliamentarian, was later killed in the siege at Lichfield in March 1643. He was shot in the forehead as he stood in front of the house (now called Brooke House) in Dam Street by a Royalist sniper, John Dyott. The shot was fired from the central spire of the cathedral.

Deprived of its custodian, Robert Greville, 2nd Lord Brooke, the castle was given into the stewardship of Major John Bridges, who was appointed Governor in 1643. A Parliamentarian garrison continued to be maintained there until 1659. In April 1660, Colonel John Hawksworth, the last governor to hold that post, was ordered by the Council of State to disband the garrison and deliver possession of the castle to Robert Greville, 4th Baron Brooke. Colonel Hawksworth had acquired Kenilworth Castle in 1650 and converted Leicester's Gatehouse into a residence for himself.

Closely linked with the castle and a major contributor to the town's cultural and social fabric is St Mary's Church. The Domesday Book tells of the 'Church of St. Mary'; however, no precise date is given for its foundation. John Rous, fifteenth-century antiquarian, who had his library at the church, states that an Anglo-Saxon mint was located east of the churchyard. The mint was established during the reign of Athelstan 924–39 and continued until the mid-twelfth century.

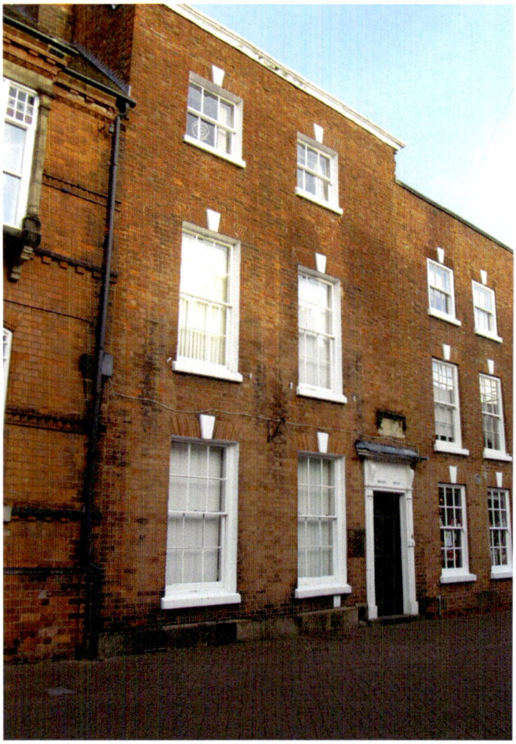

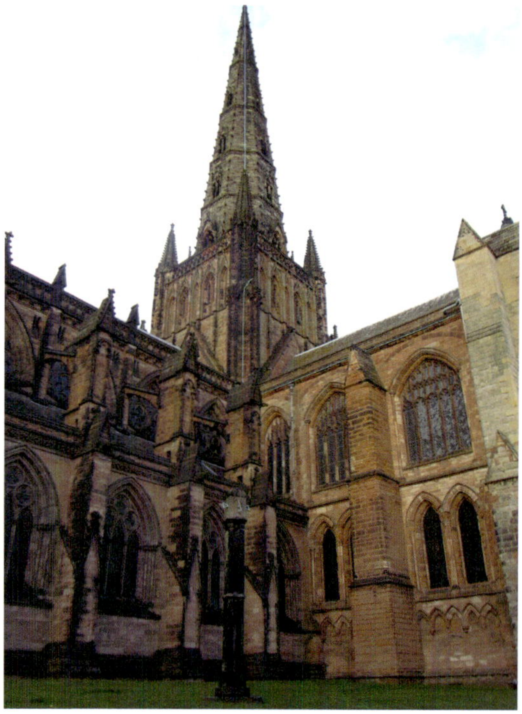

Above left: Parliamentarian Robert Greville, Lord Brooke was shot outside this house, now called Brooke House, in Dam Street, Lichfield, in 1643.

Above right: The central spire of Lichfield Cathedral, from which sniper John Dyott shot Lord Brooke in 1643.

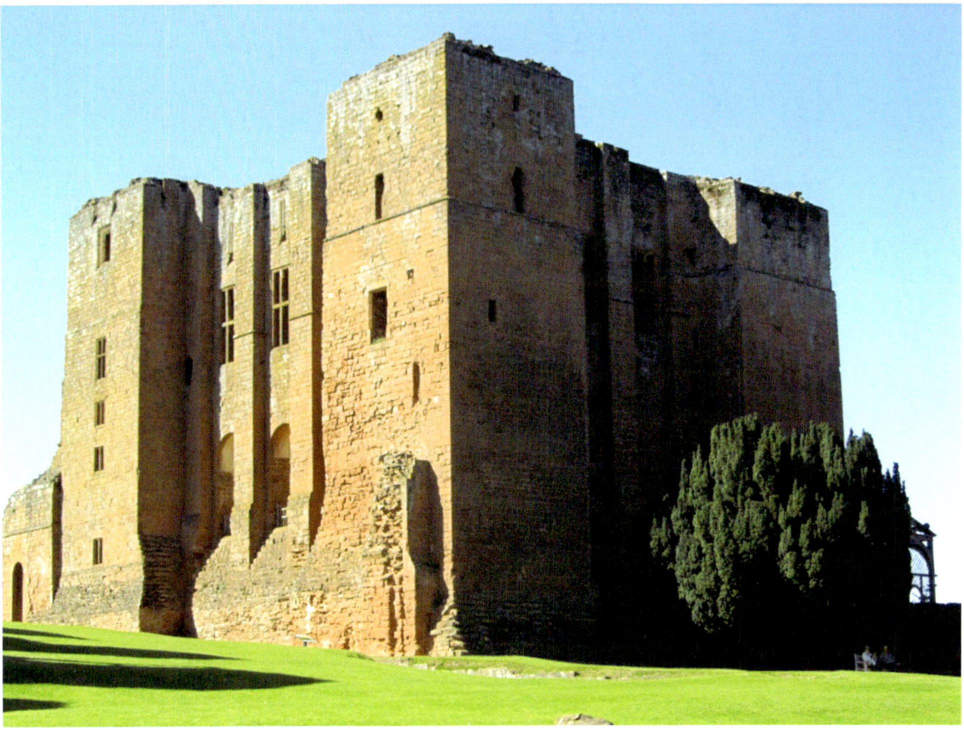

Robert Dudley, Earl of Leicester, Gatehouse, Kenilworth Castle.

It was the intention of Henry de Beaumont, the first earl of his line to establish a college of priests there, uniting it with the mother Church of All Saints which stood inside its walls. In the event this plan was carried out by his son and heir, Roger, in 1123. The college was at the same time granted seven other Warwick churches: St Nicholas, St Lawrence, St Michael, St Sepulchre, St Helen's, St John's and St Peter's.

The College belonging to St Mary's, with its dean and many priests, was suppressed under Henry VIII's Dissolution of the Monasteries. Many altars disappeared, including five nave altars commemorating saints of the churches in Warwick united with St Mary's. The extraordinary relics, which included part of the burning bush seen by Moses, also disappeared. The College building was passed into private hands after its dissolution in 1540 and was owned by the Wagstaffes of Tachbrook until 1699 when the Corporation purchased it for £260 for use as a grammar school.

When a new grammar school was built on the Myton Road in 1849, the old College, described as a beautiful building with a timbered house and square courtyard around which were passages and rooms in the form of a two-storied cloister, was sold and demolished by the purchaser – an act of civic vandalism which met with general condemnation.

By the middle of the fourteenth century St Mary's was in a very poor state of repair. The earl at that time, Thomas Beauchamp, a renowned military commander, decided to rebuild the church but died in Calais of the plague before his work came to fruition. His son, also Thomas, completed the project and the new church was finished by 1394. The elder

Thomas was buried in the chancel alongside his wife, Katherine Mortimer. Their effigies are most unusual as they are shown holding hands. Only three such examples exist.

Richard Beauchamp, Earl of Warwick, died at Rouen Castle on 30 April 1439, aged fifty-seven. In his will he left specific instructions to build a new chapel on the south side of St Mary's in Warwick to be known as the Chapel of Our Lady (now called Beauchamp Chapel). His tomb, made of Purbeck marble on which Beauchamp's effigy was placed, incorporates carvings of mourners and Warwick's emblem, the bear and ragged staff. The mourners included his son, Henry, and his wife, Cecily Neville, and notably Cecily's brother, Richard Neville, the 'Kingmaker'. Beauchamp Chapel also provided the resting place for Robert Dudley, Earl of Leicester and his infant son, Lord Denbigh, the 'Noble Impe', and for his brother, Ambrose Dudley, often referred to as the 'Good Earl of Warwick'.

The chancel, vestry and chapter house represent one of the highest peaks of English Gothic architecture. The crypt remains from the original Norman building in which there's sited a rare example of a medieval ducking stool.

During the Civil War the church was attacked by Parliamentarian Colonel Purefoy's soldiers and some stained-glass windows depicting Thomas Beckett were smashed and monuments were defaced. A cross standing at the northern end of the Market Place was also destroyed. What appears to be an act of wanton destruction was nothing of the kind as any depictions of idolatry was against the Tennent's of the Puritan laws.

St Mary's was to suffer further catastrophe when it became engulfed in flames during the Great Fire of 1694. Having escaped the fate of other buildings, the church, which was acting as a sanctuary to the people who had brought furniture and possessions to shelter from the conflagration, caught fire when their still smouldering furniture ignited. The nave and tower were destroyed, although Beauchamp Chapel was fortunately spared.

Also burnt was the library established by John Rous on an upper floor containing his books and manuscripts, most famously Rous Rolls, detailing the lives of the Earls of Warwick and King Richard III, and *Historia Regum Angliae*, which praised Henry VII and painted an unfavourable characterisation of Richard III. The library was re-established in 1701 but by that time interest had declined and didn't revive until 1895 when a library was opened by J. Merridew, printer of the *Warwick Guide*.

Rebuilding of the tower commenced at the beginning of the eighteenth century, but when it was 20 feet high above the roof, it was discovered that the two eastern piers supporting the tower showed signs of failure. It was subsequently taken down. This needed to be rebuilt and provided brothers Francis and William Smith, builder architects of Warwick, with a golden opportunity.

Plans submitted by Christopher Wren were largely ignored and rebuilding commenced to the designs of Sir William Wilson of Sutton Coldfield. Queen Anne donated £1,000 to the rebuilding of the nave and tower which was much taller than the previous one. The new tower was erected further west, supported by piers already incorporated in the west wall of the nave and on two more built out into the roadway. The 174-foot tower of this magnificent edifice now dominates the skyline.

Fires in towns were not unusual as most buildings were thatched and built using wattle and daub. Once alight, flames quickly spread from one house to another, as these were often built closely together. The effect of such calamities was well known, and it was usual

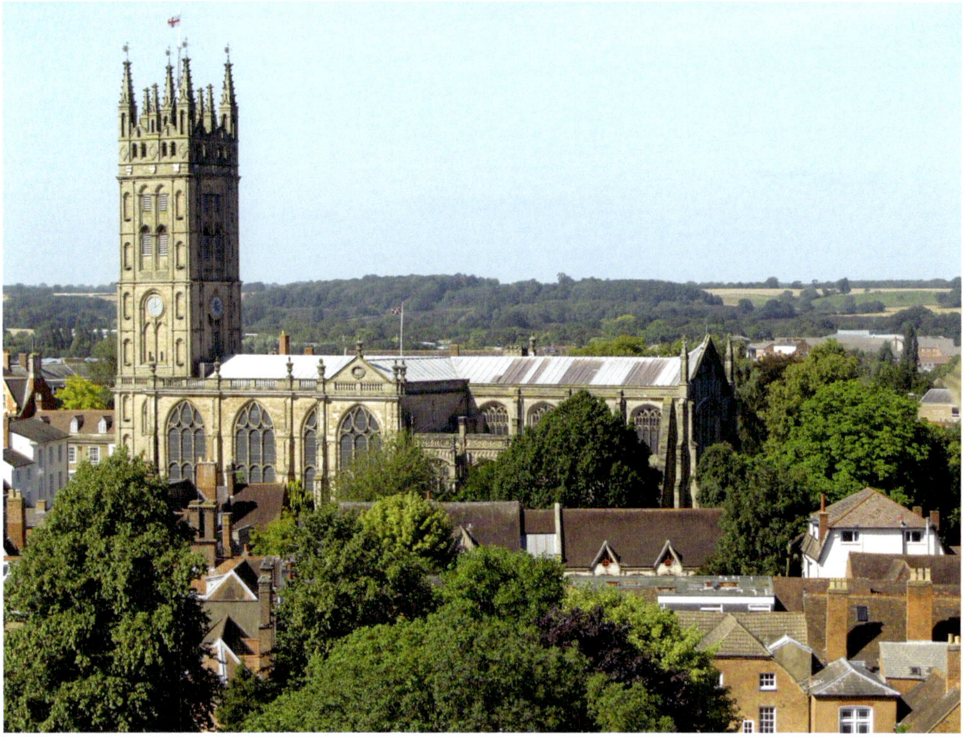

Above: St Mary's Collegiate Church and Beauchamp Chapel. This was rebuilt following the Great Fire of 1694 to the design of William Wilson, architect. Beauchamp Chapel was built on the instructions of Richard Beauchamp, Earl of Warwick.

Right: St Mary's Church. When the tower and nave were rebuilt following the Great Fire of 1694, to strengthen the tower the two supporting piers were projected into the roadway.

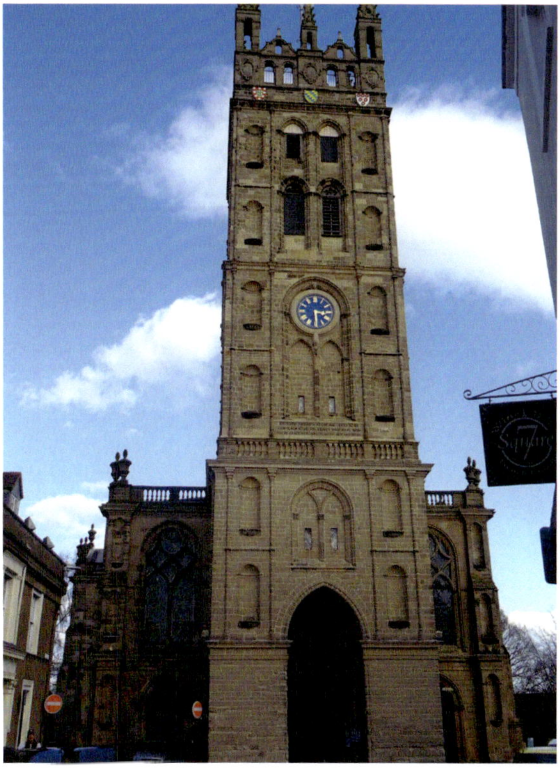

for subscriptions to be raised in neighbouring towns and on occasion all over the country. Parliament also would pass measures to aid the rebuilding of a town. As a precaution, fire buckets were sited in various places in the town to be always in readiness. Warwick benefactor Thomas Oken provided twelve leather buckets. In the event these made little difference in quelling the flames. A fire engine wasn't to be provided until the end of the seventeenth century.

The Great Fire, which probably started at the entrance to a small lane off High Pavement (Back Lane) near the Friends Meeting House, was fanned by a south-westerly breeze and soon consumed the thatch-covered buildings. It is said around 250 families lost their homes. Among the buildings destroyed by the fire was the Quaker Meeting House in High Pavement. Quaker membership in Warwick was substantial, rising from eighty-six in 1689 to between 200–300 but declining in the eighteenth century. The fire spread up Church Street and along Pebble Lane, the top of New Street and part of the Market Place. The flames also spread northwards into Sheep Street (Northgate Street) and consumed several houses in the Butts.

One building that escaped the flames in the Market Place was the Church of St John. This was shown in 1654 as a small building without a tower to the south of the Booth Hall and was for a time to house the King's Grammar School. It appears to have been demolished before 1711.

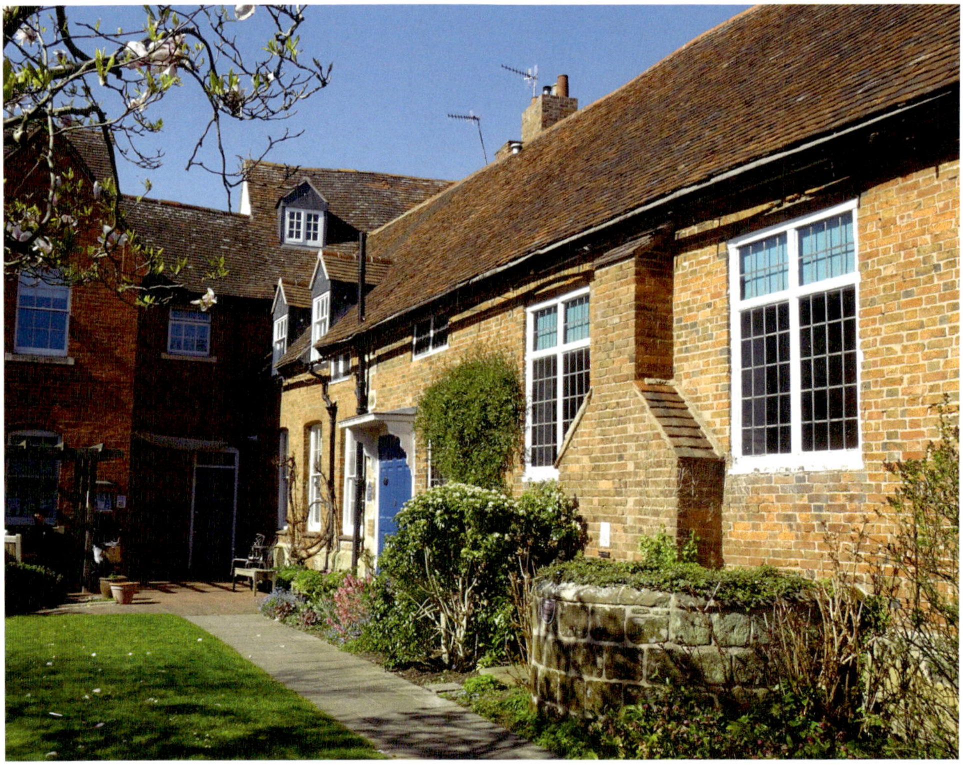

Friends Meeting House, High Street (High Pavement). The garden was once a burial ground for Quakers and is now open to the public.

The damage to Warwick was estimated to be valued at £120,000 for the rebuilding of High Street, part of Jury Street, Church Street and the area around St Mary's. Nearly 300 people, of whom 156 were tradesmen, applied to the Commissioners for relief for the rebuilding of their premises. One of the Commissioners was Lord Brooke who was said to have influenced the remodelling of the town as a 'fashionable antechamber' for the castle.

The day after the fire, Lord Brooke and other wealthy people moved swiftly to mitigate its disastrous effects on the populace and started a subscription fund to cover peoples' losses. Nearly £900 was collected from individuals, cities and boroughs. The Treasury made a grant of £400 per year and 1,000 tons of timber. The misery caused by the fire was further compounded with serious food shortages at that time. The justices immediately took steps to prevent a repetition of the fire by demanding the replacement of thatched roofs by tiles on 200 barns, stables and hovels.

A survey of the properties of east and west in 1590 and John Speed's plan of the town drawn *c.* 1610 shows within the line of the medieval walls, particularly High Street, Jury Street and Castle Street, houses were built closely together. They were easy prey for the flames and were quickly consumed by the fire; whereas those outside the town walls were less closely built together and interspersed with barns, gardens and crofts. Many barns and cottages were in Hoggesford, Saltisford and Wallditch. Crofts were to be found in Friar Lane and gardens in Linen Hill.

The Great Fire proved a significant change in the fortunes of the town by shedding the medieval timber-built and thatched structures which enabled a more attractive town to emerge. Reconstruction of Warwick, arising from the ashes, gave it a gentrified air with buildings constructed with brick and stone in the style of William and Mary.

Impetus to rebuilding the town in a gentrified style produced several individuals whose work as architects and builders had earned them a wide reputation. Among them was Francis Smith and Francis Hiorne. Francis Hiorne was three times Mayor of Warwick and County Bridgemaster.

The stone for rebuilding the town after the fire may have come from a quarry located in Bowling Green Street. This was the site of several quarry pits dating to the post medieval period. The pits were located 400 metres north-west of Warwick Castle. Other quarry site locations were St Mary's churchyard and behind New Street (Horse Cheaping).

The Book of Warwick records that 'Smith of Warwick', as Francis was more commonly known, was a client's ideal contractor due to his famous honesty and reliability, able to deliver buildings on time and on budget. Born in 1672 at Tettenhall near Wolverhampton, Francis and brother William arrived in Warwick following the disastrous fire. Francis set up his masonry business in Marble Yard and helped William rebuild St Mary's. Together they were probably responsible for restoring much of the damage done to the town under the auspices of architect Thomas Archer.

Francis's reputation spread among the Midlands gentry and aristocracy, with almost all his works within a 50-mile radius of Warwick. Attributed to his own definitive style of architecture were the Court House in Warwick, a handsome rectory at Hampton Lucy, the earliest part of Compton Verney, Umberslade Hall and part of Abington Hall, Northampton among others.

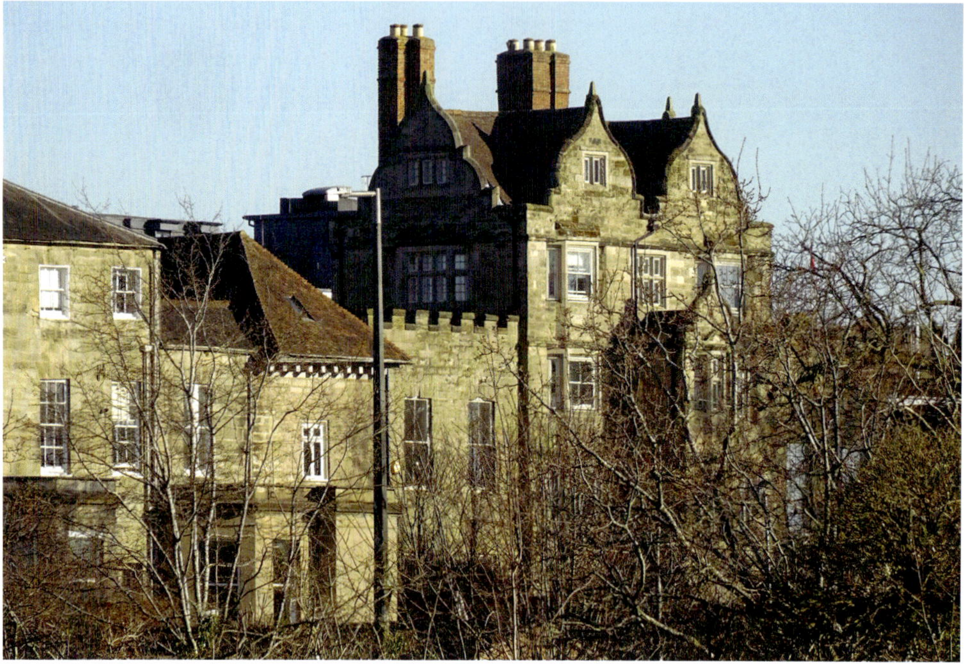

Marble House, Grade II Jacobean House, built *c.* 1650. This was the accommodation of Francis Smith, who together with brother William helped rebuild the town following the Great Fire of 1694.

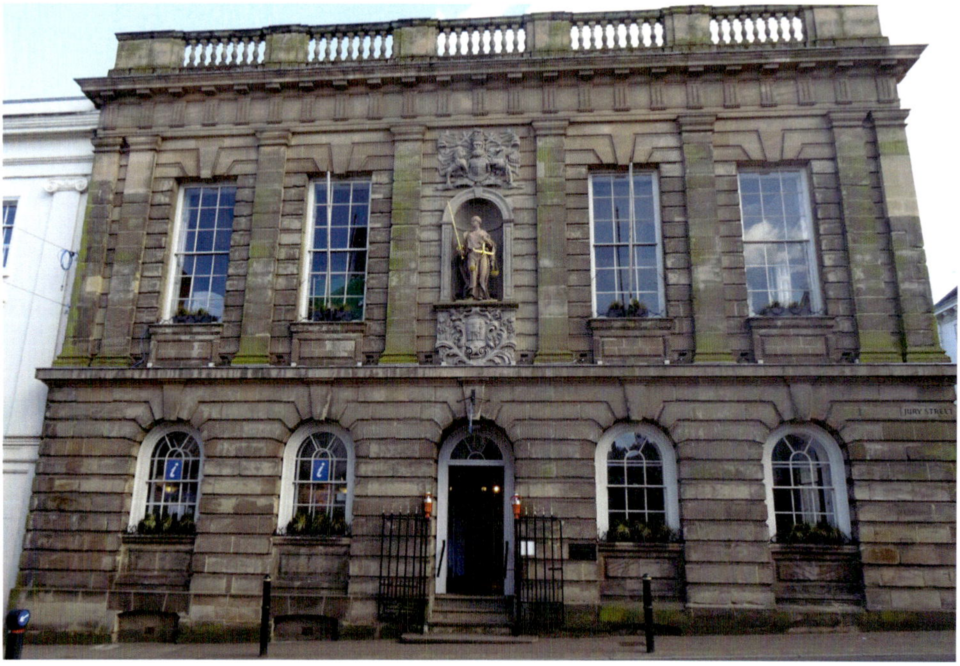

The Court House. Designed and built by Francis Smith in 1725, this replaced the earlier building which escaped being burned down in the Great Fire, except for the Mayor's Parlour. It was once the site of St Peter's Chapel.

Having settled in the town and carved a distinguished career during which time he was created Mayor of Warwick twice, the indefatigable Francis Smith died in April 1738. No memorial marks his burial place in St Mary's, but Francis had put up a tablet to his brother William who died at Tettenhall in 1724.

Rebuilding of the town by its architect builders Francis and William Smith and Francis Hiorne presented it as the residence of the gentry. The *Victoria County History - Vol. 8* states that the social change was reflected in the trading community by the appearance at the end of the eighteenth century of hairdressers, stay makers, pattern makers, gardeners, a perfumer, a coach painter, a nursery and seedsman. Celia Fiennes, visiting Warwick *c.* 1700, says:

> Its most new buildings which is with brick and coyn'd with stone and the windows the same; there still remains some few houses of the old town which are all built of stone; the streets are very handsome and the buildings regular and fine, not very lofty being limited by Act of Parliament to build the town.

The town that had emerged from the ashes was described by Daniel Defoe in 1716 as 'now rebuilt in so noble and so beautiful manner that few towns in England make so fine an appearance'.

The castle, which had been fortunate to escape the devastation of the fire, saw Francis Greville, 8th Baron Brooke come into possession of it and its estates in 1740. He began a programme of major works on the castle and grounds. In 1750 Lancelot 'Capability' Brown was engaged to lay out the grounds at the castle which covered some 64 acres. He was head gardener at Stowe, Buckinghamshire, and had yet to establish his reputation as the main architect of the English landscape garden.

'Capability' was requisitioned by Lord Brooke to give the castle a more natural connection with the River Avon. In his inimitable style, which was to become his trademark, Brown simplified the long narrow stretch by sweeping it into a lawn that dropped right to the riverbank, stopped at each end by bold clumps of native trees. A sinuous winding drive was cut through the rock to give an impression of greater distance between the front gates and the castle entrance. Landscapes were not the only string to Capability's bow; he was also a competent architect and in 1753–55 rebuilt the porch and stairway to the Great Hall.

Francis Greville was also fortunate to be introduced to the famous Italian painter Canaletto by his cousin's husband, the Duke of Northumberland, who was his patron. Greville had probably become familiar with Canaletto's work on his Grand Tour of Europe where he no doubt spent time in Italy. Canaletto was commissioned to do paintings of the castle, and he produced five oil paintings and five pen drawings which also included parts of the town. The well-known view of the east front of the castle is little changed to this present day, although the surrounding landscape has altered.

The Great Bridge, with fourteen arches over the fast-flowing Avon from Bridge End to below the castle walls, was falling into decay in the latter half of the eighteenth century. This narrow bridge conveyed wagons and horses, soldiers, tradesmen and people entering the town. The noise generated by this influx wasn't appreciated by George Greville, 2nd

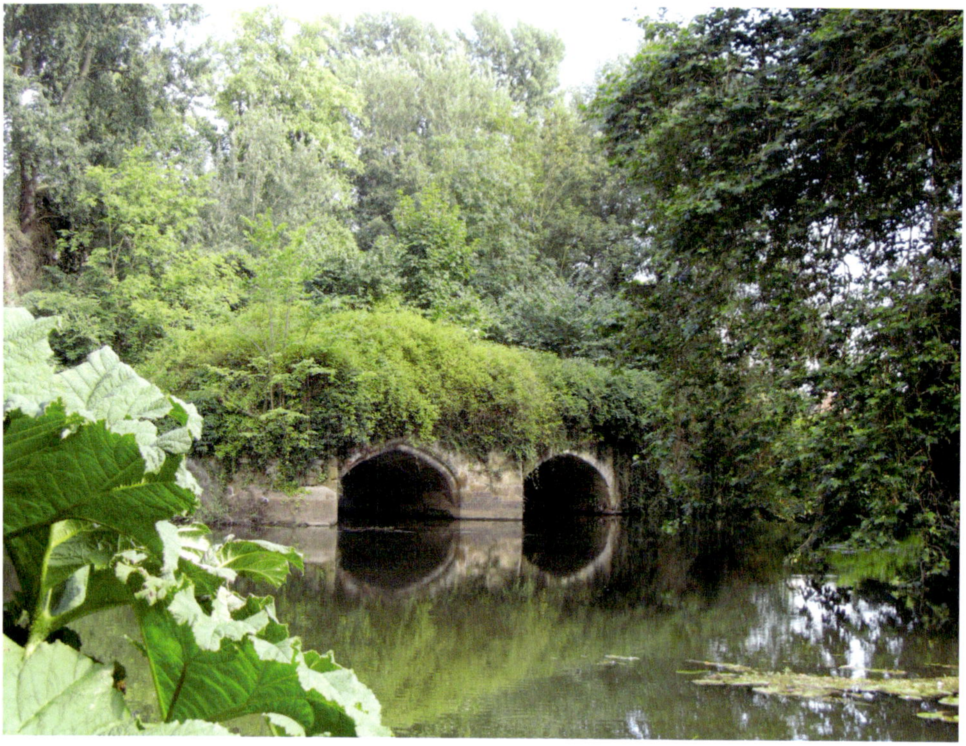

The ruins of the thirteenth-century Great Bridge which originally provided a crossing over the River Avon for people entering the town. The remains of the decayed bridge were later carried away by floods in 1795.

Earl of Warwick. He decided he would prefer another bridge to be built further upstream to carry the traffic and noise away from immediately below the castle walls and so the services of William Eborall, a local mason and architect, were engaged.

George Greville also commissioned William Eborall to build a conservatory in 1786 in the grounds to house the magnificent Warwick Vase. The earl acquired the vase from his uncle, William Hamilton, who was Ambassador to the Court of Naples. Hamilton discovered the white marble vase, thought to date from the fourth century BC, in 1770 at the bottom of a small lake called Pantanello overlooking the Vale of Tempe, near Tivoli. It was reputed to be capable of holding 163 gallons and measured 5'6" high and 5'8" in diameter.

A New Bridge was constructed with a single arch, being 100 ft span and cost £4,000. It was opened in 1793. The Corporation paid a quarter towards the cost and the earl contributed the rest. Shortly afterwards in 1795 the Great Bridge, referred to as early as 1208, was partly swept away by floods, leaving a ruin which presents a picturesque photo opportunity to this day. The result of moving the bridge to convey traffic from the Myton and Banbury Roads into the town led to Bridge End and Mill Street becoming redundant as major thoroughfares. Bridge End especially became severed from the town and virtually became a small hamlet with its collection of pretty cottages. The earl also

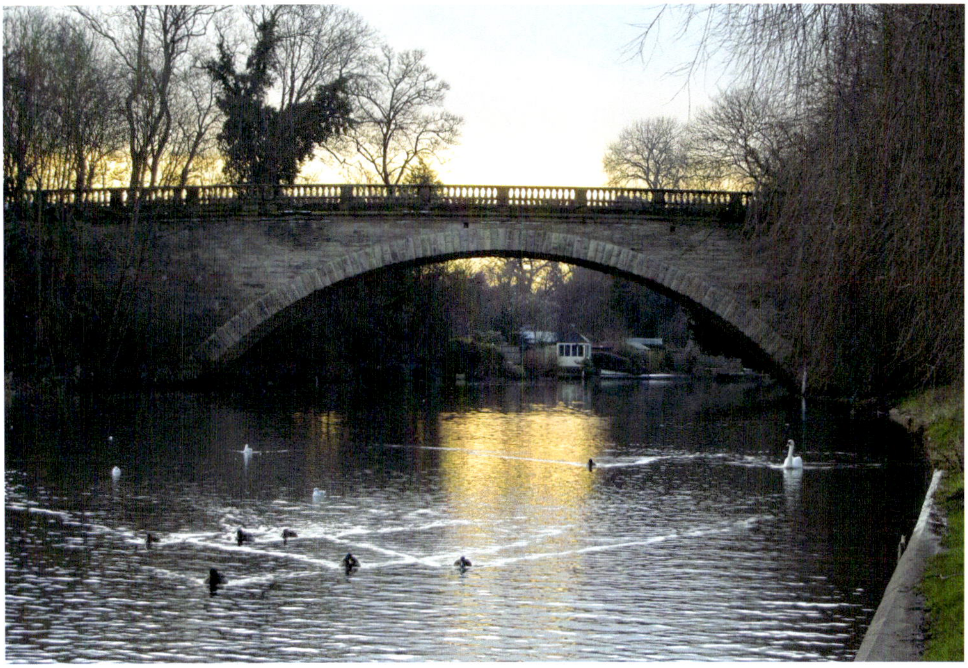

The New Bridge was constructed by William Eborall in 1793, with a 100-foot single span and cost £4,000.

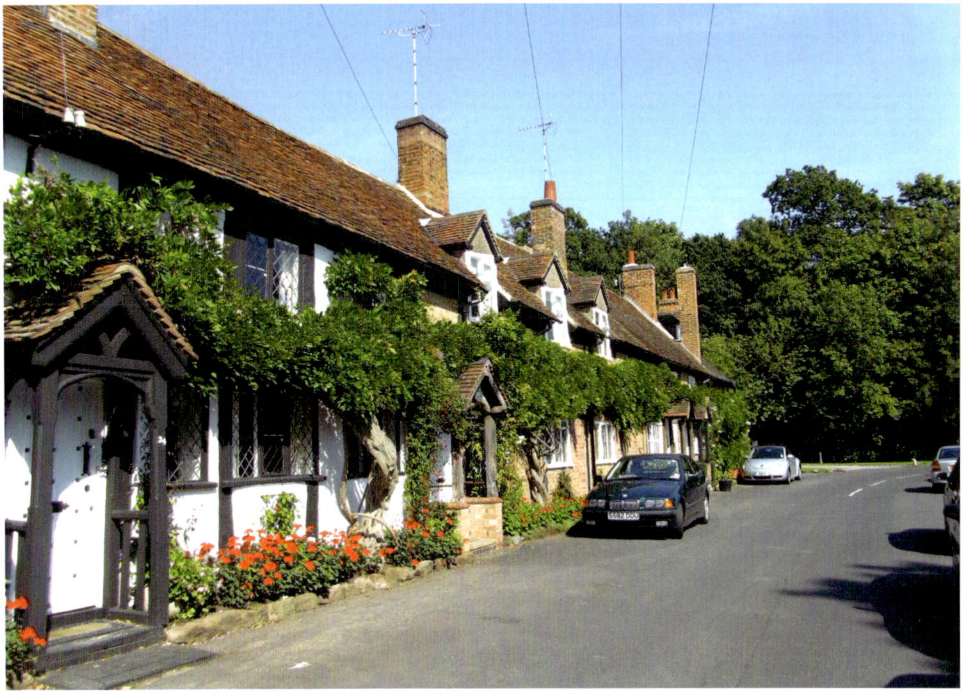

Bridge End. This became redundant as a major thoroughfare into the town when the New Bridge was constructed further upstream.

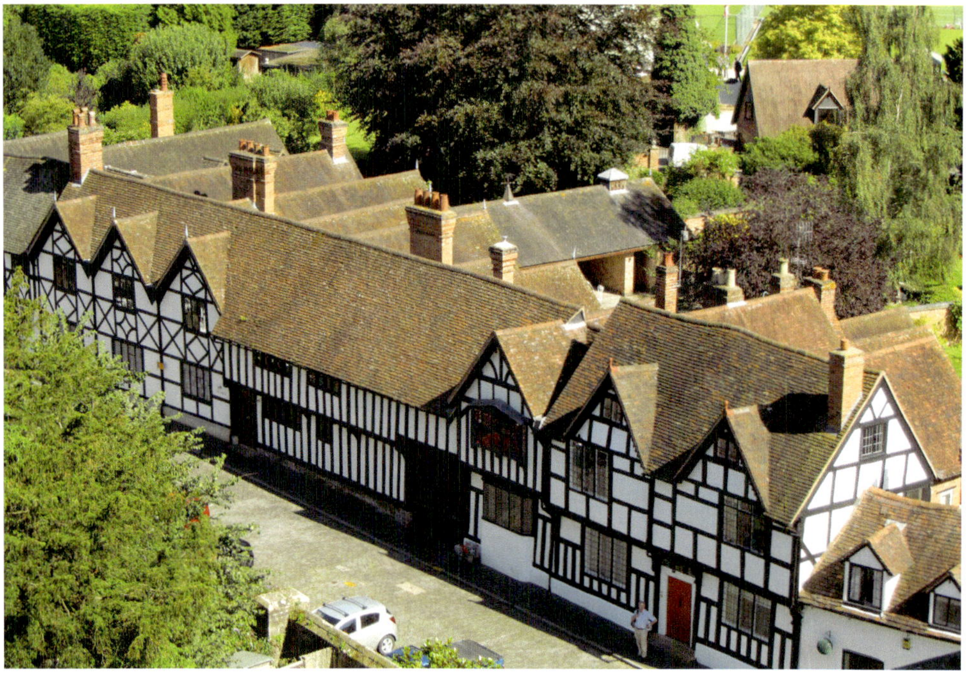

Mill Street. This street adjacent to the castle also became redundant as a major thoroughfare into the town when New Bridge was built in 1793 on the wishes of Earl George Greville to take away the noise of traffic from immediately below the castle walls.

extended the castle grounds by enclosing more land with a high wall, planting more trees and with the ruined bridge now defunct, was able to distance the castle from the town.

The River Avon had been unnavigable up to Warwick despite attempts to make it navigable, which restricted trade and commerce to the locality. Richard Beauchamp had attempted to make it navigable in the 1400s by suggesting that the waters should be deepened between Tewkesbury and Warwick, but this plan was never acted upon.

Elizabethan John Fisher in *The Black Book of Warwick* reveals there was a lack of manufacturers, with the mercers, who included the town's benefactor Thomas Oken, selling linen and spices, with many folks engaged in husbandry. Agriculture was prominent in the economy of Warwick. There were open arable fields around three of the suburban settlements and extensive meadow and pastureland, especially in the earl's manor. To the north-west were the woods and pastures of Wedgnock Park. The River Avon was of value for its fisheries which always belonged to the earl's manor. The value of the fisheries in 1268 was £1.6s and in 1369 £3.6s.

Due to its poor communications and its proximity to industrial Coventry, the economic position of Warwick showed little change between the fifteenth and eighteenth centuries, with mercers, drapers and malting among the most prosperous trades. This was to change with the building of canals and the Napoleonic Wars which brought large-scale industry to Warwick. An Act of Parliament in 1793 supported by the Earl of Warwick was passed authorising the Birmingham to Warwick canal and Warwick and Napton canal in 1800.

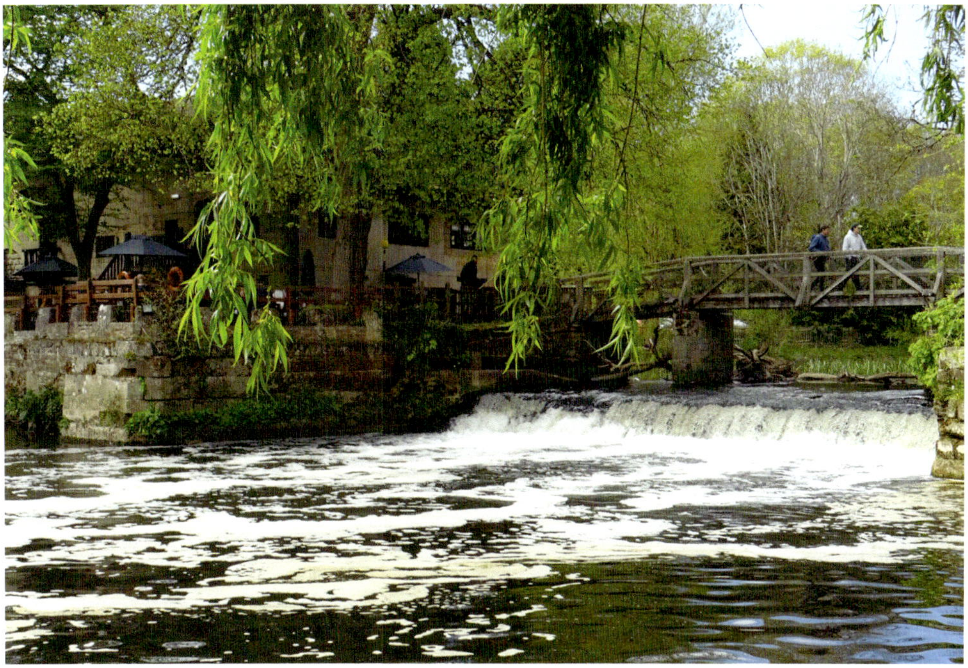

The River Avon was unnavigable up to Warwick and restricted trade and commerce to the locality in the sixteenth and seventeenth centuries until the building of the canals.

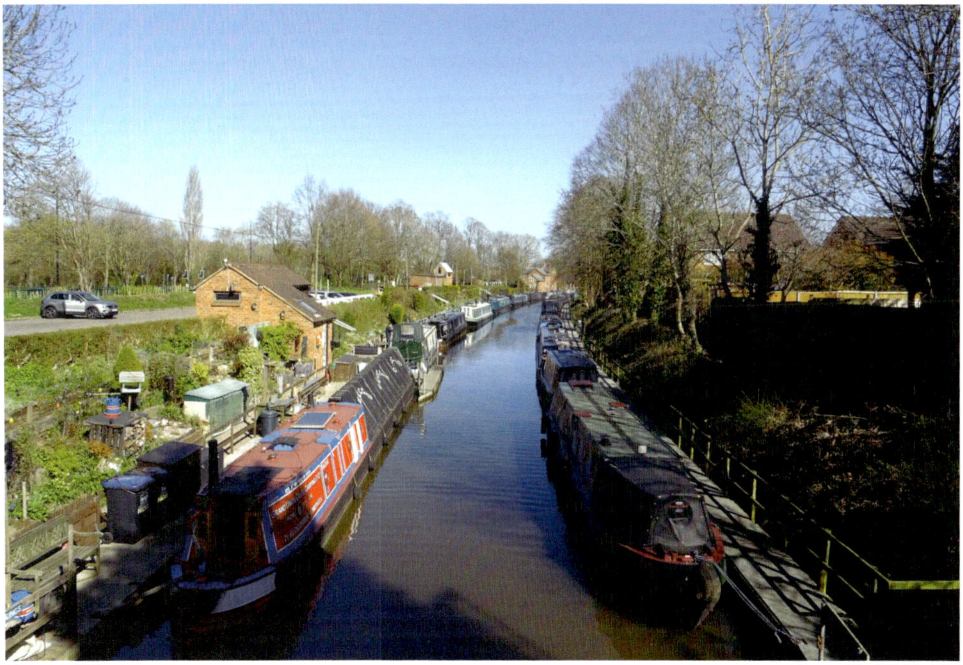

The Great Union Canal, previously the Birmingham to Warwick Canal. This enabled the transport of cargo, mainly coal which powered textile industries in the 1790s and early 1800s and the gasworks in 1822.

PART II

Development of Warwick as a County Town

The canals saw a mini boom in manufacturing during the first two decades of the nineteenth century. This was part of the wider Industrial Revolution then taking place. The immediate effect of the canal system was to reduce the price of coal so that for the first time it became possible to set up relatively large-scale industry in small country towns, well away from the coalfields. A wharf established in the Saltisford stimulated industrial development and by 1851 the area next to the wharf was occupied by timber yards, coal yards, and goods yards as well as several pubs and a new gasworks. The wharf survived in part until 1969 but had been filled in by 1983.

Although worsted and woollen cloth had been produced as a cottage industry on a considerable scale at the beginning of the eighteenth century, it wasn't until the arrival of the canal system that factories were established. Textiles industries were to flourish in Warwick when William Parkes and brother Joseph set up workshops and warehouses in Barrack Street in 1789. In 1795 they formed a partnership with Joseph Brookhouse, cotton spinner, and Samuel Crompton. They built their factory in the Saltisford in 1796 for worsted spinning and by 1815 it employed 500 hands. The chief markets were Leicester, Hinkley and Nottingham for worsted and Kidderminster for yarn. William Parkes took up residence in Marble House which had also been owned by Francis Smith.

In 1792 Messrs Smart set up a cotton-spinning factory at Emscote, employing around 50 hands, using water and steam. The finished spun was sent to Manchester. Messrs Parker, cotton weavers, opened a factory in Oil Mill Lane (Priory Road) and employed 200 hands. By 1815 many more business had been established. These included Messrs Lamb of Market Place, hatters, Tomes and Handley's Navigation Mill, Nunn, Brown and Freeman's lace factory and Thomas Roberts iron foundry.

This boom however was short-lived. The businesses of Parkes, Brookhouse and Crompton collapsed in 1819 following the signing of the Paris Peace Treaty in 1815 which ended the Napoleonic Wars. Smarts and Parker had also disappeared by 1822. Lamb, the hatters who took over Parkes factory in 1819, were not included in Pigots Commercial Directory for 1841. Trades other than textiles sprang up in their place such as Mollady's hat factory in the Saltisford and William Holland's stained-glass and decorative painting establishment at St John's.

Parkes was later to have a street named after him. Also adjoining Parkes Street was Wallace Street which had an unusual origin. In 1825 a lion called Wallace was procured by William Wombwell, a circus owner, to fight two bulldogs in the Factory Yard off the Saltisford. Wallace put up such a good fight, killing both dogs to the delight of the

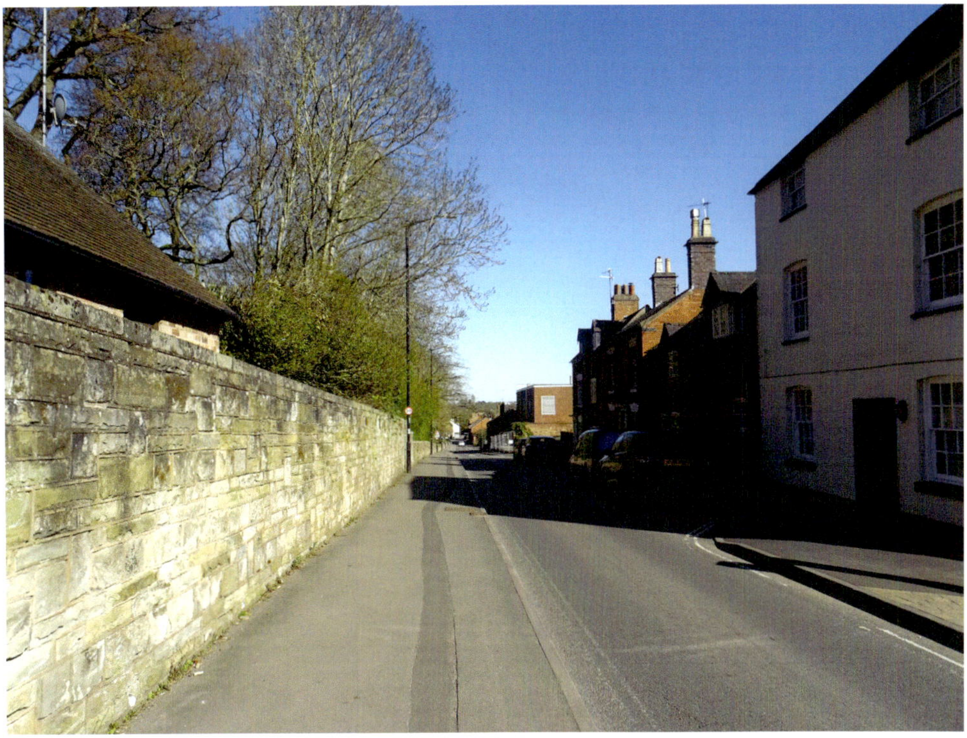

Priory Road (Previously Dog Lane and Oil Mill Lane). Messrs Parker, cotton weavers, set up a factory here in the early 1800s employing 200 hands.

onlookers, that a Street was named after him and a tavern. Wallace Street was the site of a large brewery, Jaggard, Jaggard & Hiorns, and Messrs Lamb's Hat manufactory. The name of this street was to disappear however when it was demolished in the twentieth century.

As modes of entertainment, bloodsports were popular, lion baiting being just one of the attractions at this time. Others included bear baiting, cockfighting and cock throwing. Cock throwing involved tethering the unfortunate bird to a stake and throwing missiles at it. The venue for cockfighting was a building in Smith Street, behind the former Volunteer, later Cavalier Public House, and previously a malting house in the sixteenth century. The two-storey building had a cockfighting pit upstairs with rows of terraced benches round it.

Throwing missiles at cocks wasn't the only diversion afforded to the populace. The stocks and pillory also provided for those inclined to leer and jeer at the helpless victim. *The Book of Warwick* records that in 1687 Marmaduke Malin, sentenced for perjury, had 'to stand in the pillory and have his ears nailed to it'. The stocks were situated in the Market Hall (now Museum).

Our Warwickshire records that in the centre of High Market in an area known as the Barley Market was the Booth Hall or Tolbooth. Stalls were rented to traders until 1505 when it became the residence of the manorial bailiff. In 1554 it was given to the newly created corporation. As a result of a petition to the Corporation that the Booth Hall was inadequate, a committee was set up early in 1670 to bargain for stone to erect a Market Hall.

The building of the Market Hall was supervised by William Hurlbutt in the seventeenth century. It originally had open arches to the ground floor which sheltered stalls from the elements. It served a multiplicity of purposes. Part of one floor was let as a leather hall; various tradesmen were accommodated and it also served as a store for ammunition and accoutrements of the militia. The 'Black Hole' held felons due to appear before the magistrates. Warwick Museum records that thirteen people were incarcerated at one time in a space barely big enough for a full-grown tiger to stretch out. Debtors were incarcerated upstairs where the caretaker had his quarters.

At the beginning of the nineteenth century a palisade of iron railings was placed between the piers supporting the arches of the Market Hall and later the stocks, which had previously stood to the north of the Market Hall, was replaced by some on wheels. To add to the humiliation and indignity of the miscreant, he had to drag the stocks and place them within the railings. The stocks were mainly used for drunkenness and were abolished in 1872.

An incident witnessed by a bystander on one occasion provided an amusing diversion. A small boy, urged by his mother, crept under the rail separating the crowd when the police warden wasn't looking and gave the fellow in the stocks a bottle of water (or possibly something stronger), which he hid under his jacket. When the warden's back was turned the fellow would take out the bottle and have a swig, to the amusement of the onlookers.

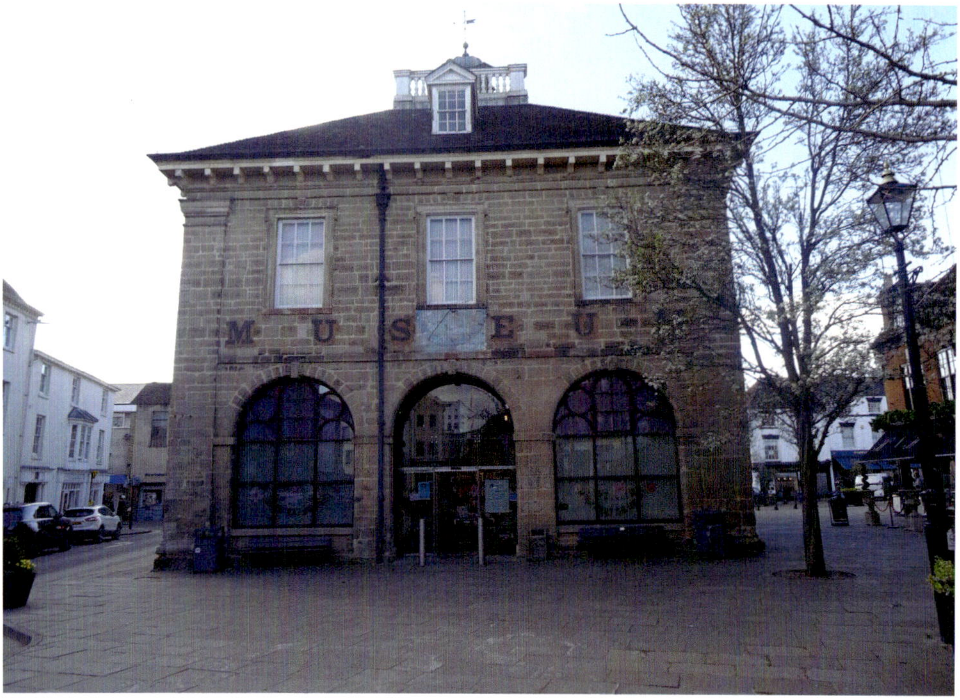

Warwick Museum, once a Booth Hall with open arches accommodating stalls. It was established as a natural history and archaeological museum in 1836. A bell was cast to hang in the cupola in 1694. It was moved to Warwick School in the nineteenth century.

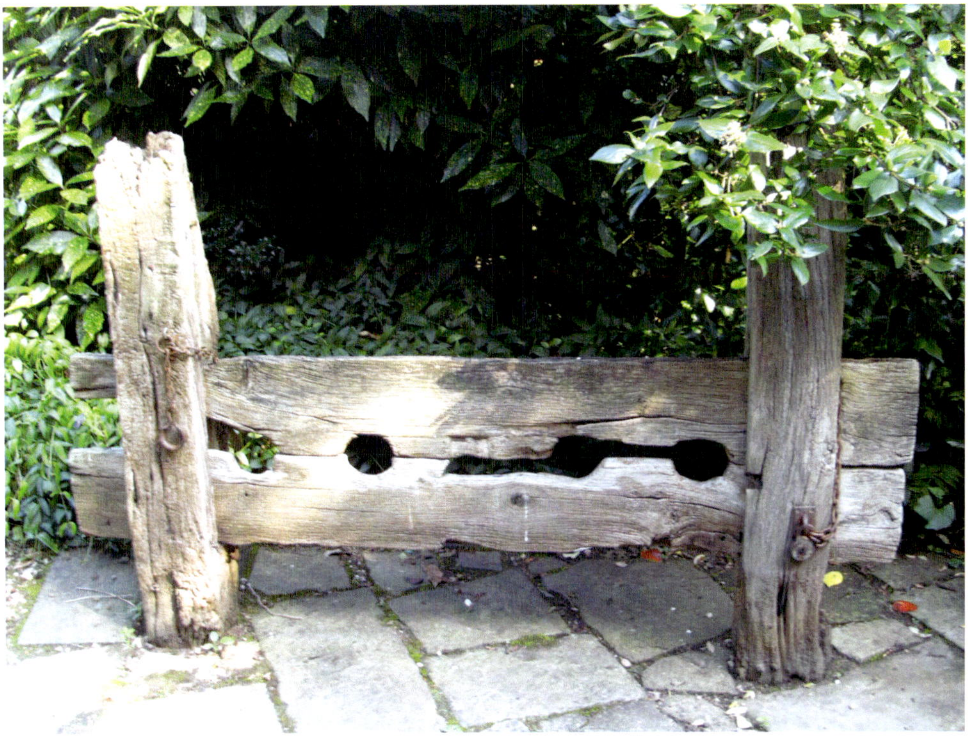

The stocks were once located in the Market Hall (Museum) and used mainly for drunkenness. They were abolished in 1872.

The Market Hall also served as a venue for the justices while a new Shire Hall was being built in 1753–58. This was to the designs of architect Sanderson Miller and the builders were William and David Hiorn of Warwick. Adjacent the Shire Hall the former gaol was enlarged between 1779 and 1783 by Thomas Johnson. A new House of Correction was built, designed and executed by Henry Couchman between 1784 and 1787. The cramped conditions of the gaol however were far from humane, and a new gaol was built with better facilities on the Cape, north of Warwick, in 1860.

It was in the courtroom in the Shire Hall that a sensational case was heard at the Quarter Sessions by Justice Francis Buller in March 1781. Captain John Donellan, a former soldier of the East India Company, cashiered and Master of Ceremonies at the Pantheon in London, was convicted for the murder by poisoning of his brother-in-law, twenty-year-old Theodosius Bourton, Baronet of Lawford Hall, near Rugby. Captain Donellan was hanged at Warwick on 2 April 1781. He was probably conveyed to the gallows along Gaol Hall Lane (Gerrard Street) and Warytree Street. Afterwards his body was taken to the Court House for dissection.

The Book of Warwick records that at St Nicholas Church in 1604, ringing the bell 'for a prisoner and for the beare (bier) to the Jubett' cost one shilling, and there was a payment in 1615 for bell and bier for 'Mr Throgemarten' (Throckmorton) who also perished on the scaffold across the river.

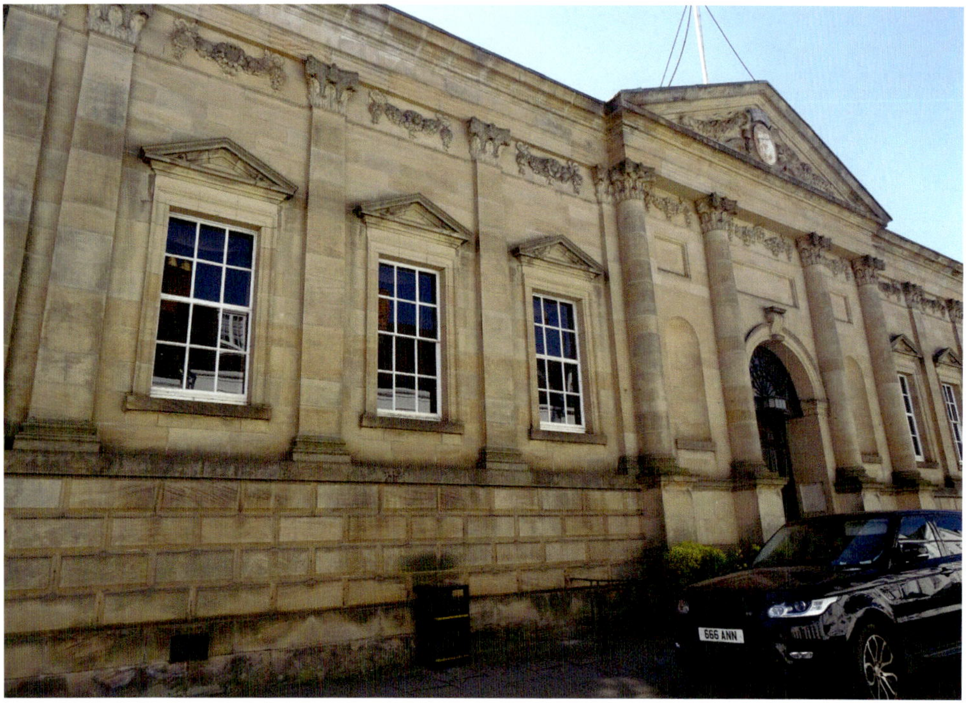

The Shire Hall, built in 1753–58. The whole magnificent façade is completed with Greek Doric columns supporting an entablature with a triglyph frieze.

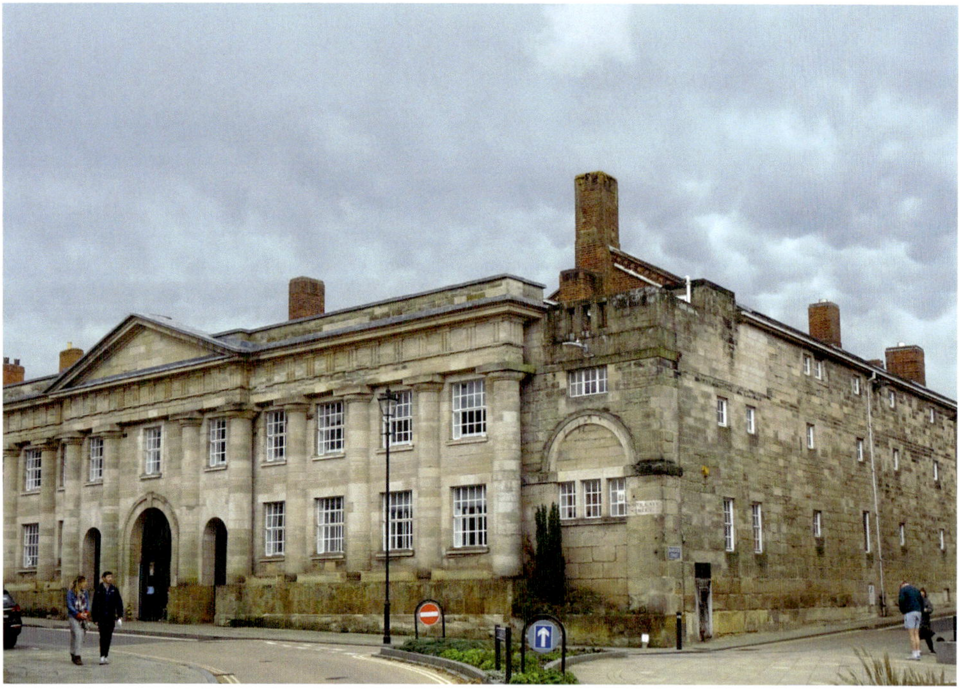

The long two-storied gaol designed by Thomas Johnson, built in 1779–83.

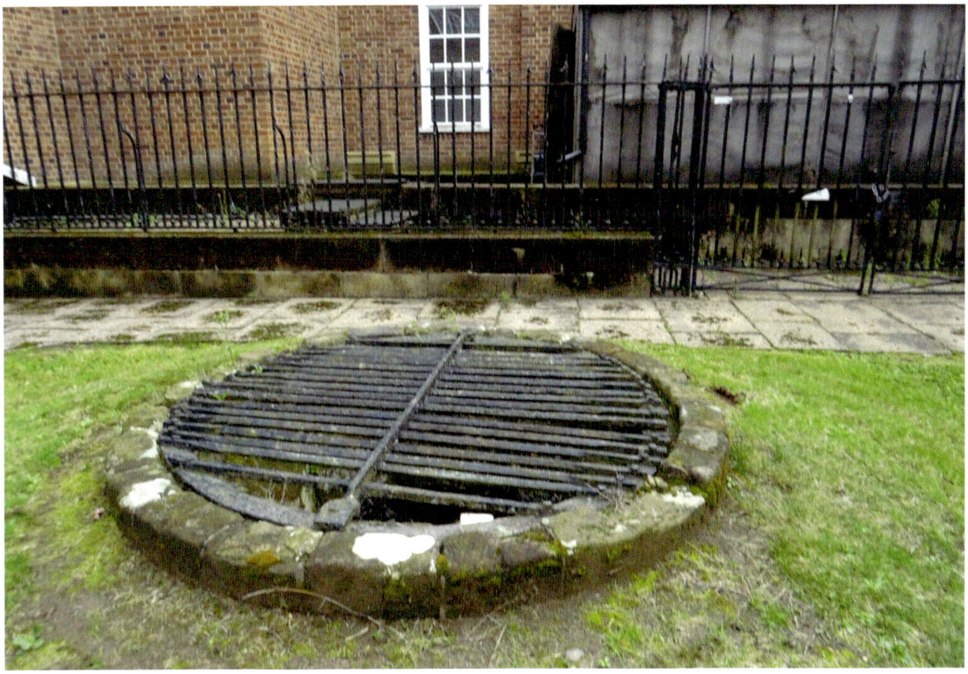

The cover of the dungeon is directly above the cesspit. It was used for incarcerating prisoners overnight. Initially these were Quakers and then deserters from the Napoleonic Wars. Its use declined in the latter eighteenth century.

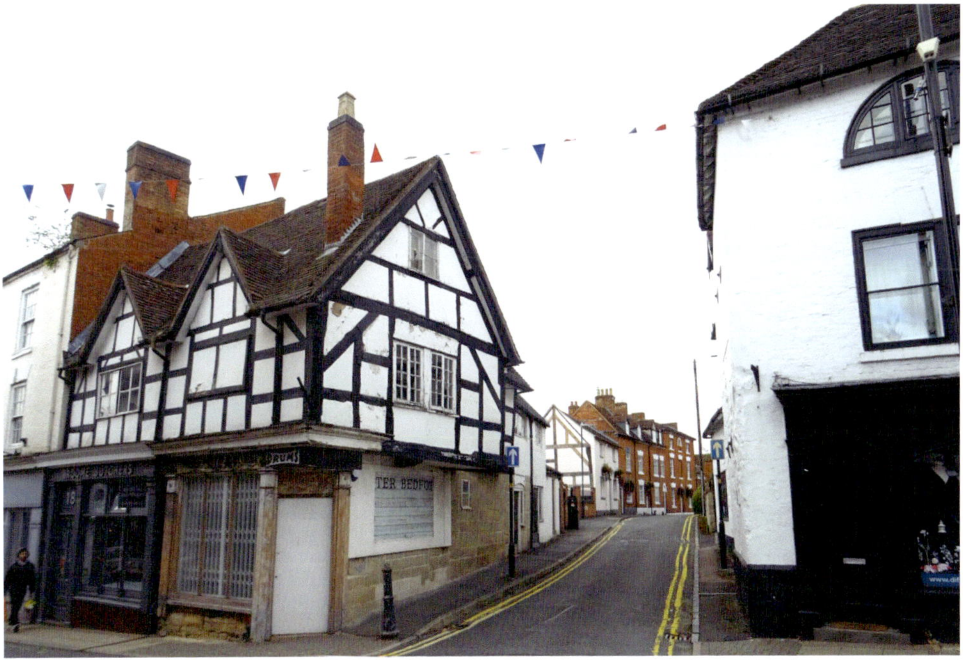

Gerrard Street (Gaol Hall Lane) felons would have been conveyed through Gaol Hall Lane and Warytree Street to the gallows on Gallows Hill, Banbury Road.

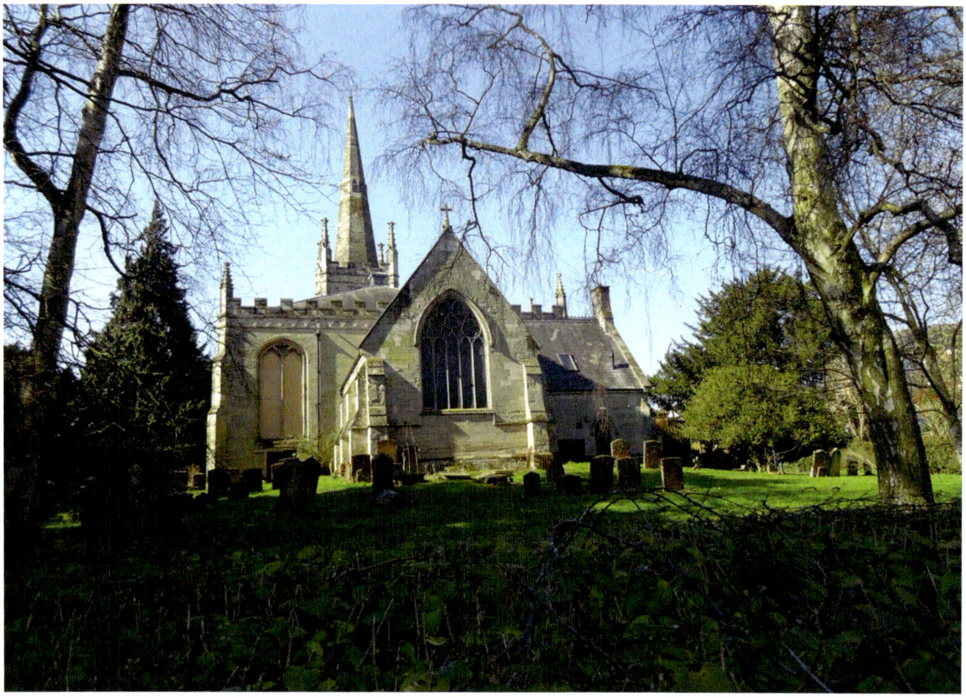

St Nicholas Church was built on the site of a medieval church and Saxon nunnery in 1795.

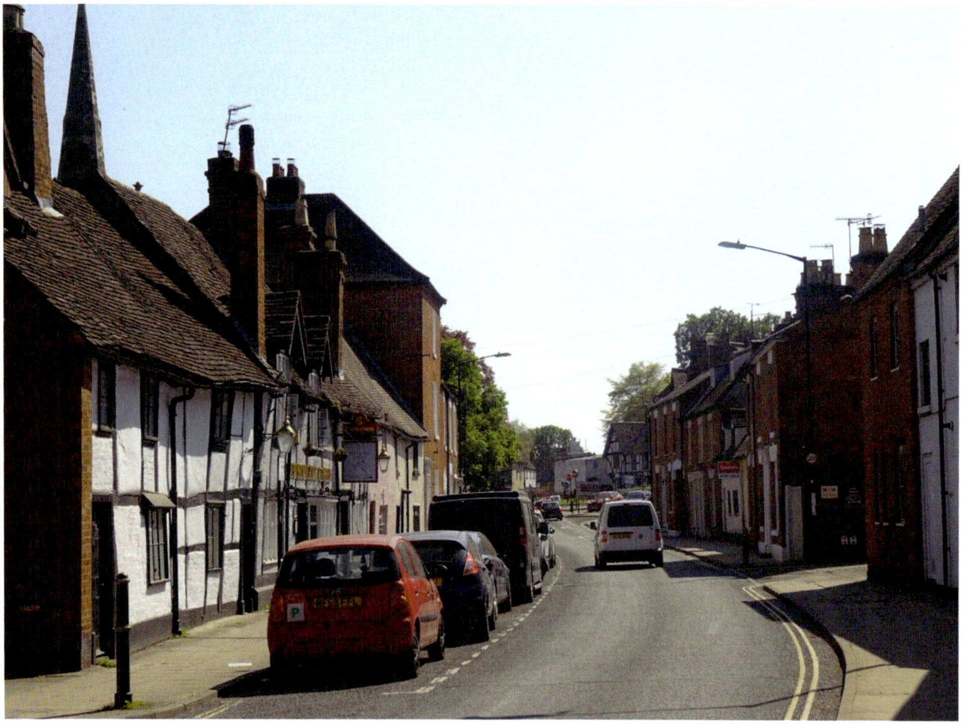

St Nicholas Church Street.

St Nicholas Church, having strong links with the castle and St Mary's Church, was built *c*. 1785 by Thomas Johnson in the Gothic style and replaced a decaying medieval church. Its Saxon roots lay in a former nunnery on the site. It has been suggested that the incumbents of both churches may also have been chaplains to the Earls of Warwick and owed their appointments to their influence. The parishes of St Nicholas and St Mary were the only two in the borough until the nineteenth century.

Bloodsports and leering at the unfortunates held in the pillory or the stocks or even witnessing public hangings wasn't the only forms of diversion available. Fairs, markets and theatre also provided for kindlier forms of entertainment. Eighteenth-century Warwick was a bustling market town with a variety of fairs and markets that played a crucial role in its economy and social life. Weekly markets featured a range of goods, including food, livestock and various crafts. The development of specialised markets saw separate markets created for the sale of corn, cheese and cattle, rather like the farmer's and French markets held today. The regulation and organisation of these markets was overseen by local authorities.

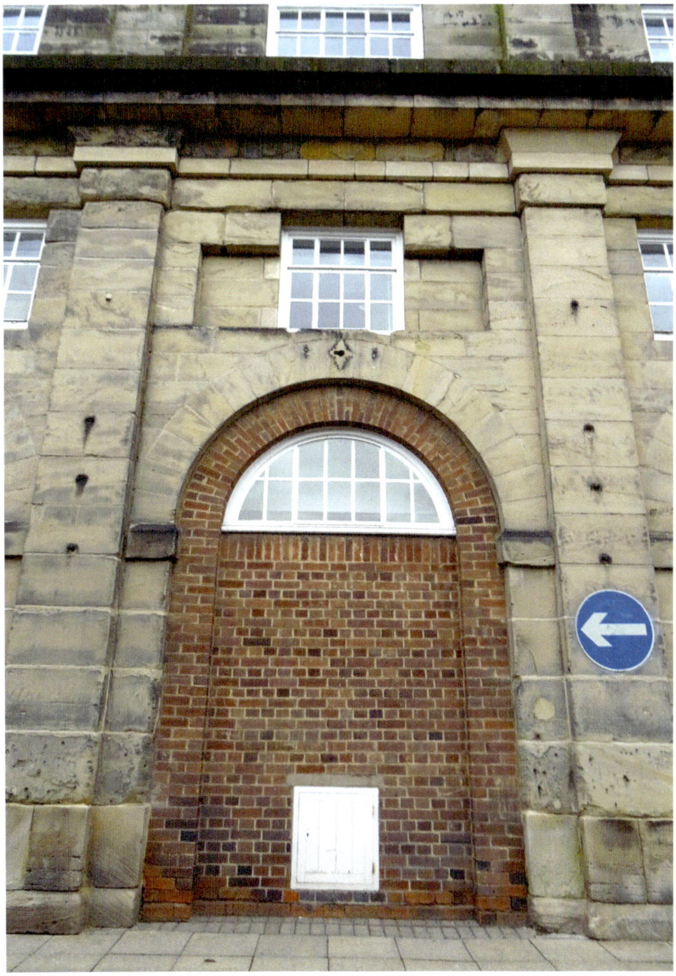

Barrack Street (Wallditch, later Bridewell Street). Felons were hanged outside this gate. Marks of the gibbet are still visible and rings on either side of the gate are embedded in the wall. These secured chains which stretched across the road and held the public at bay.

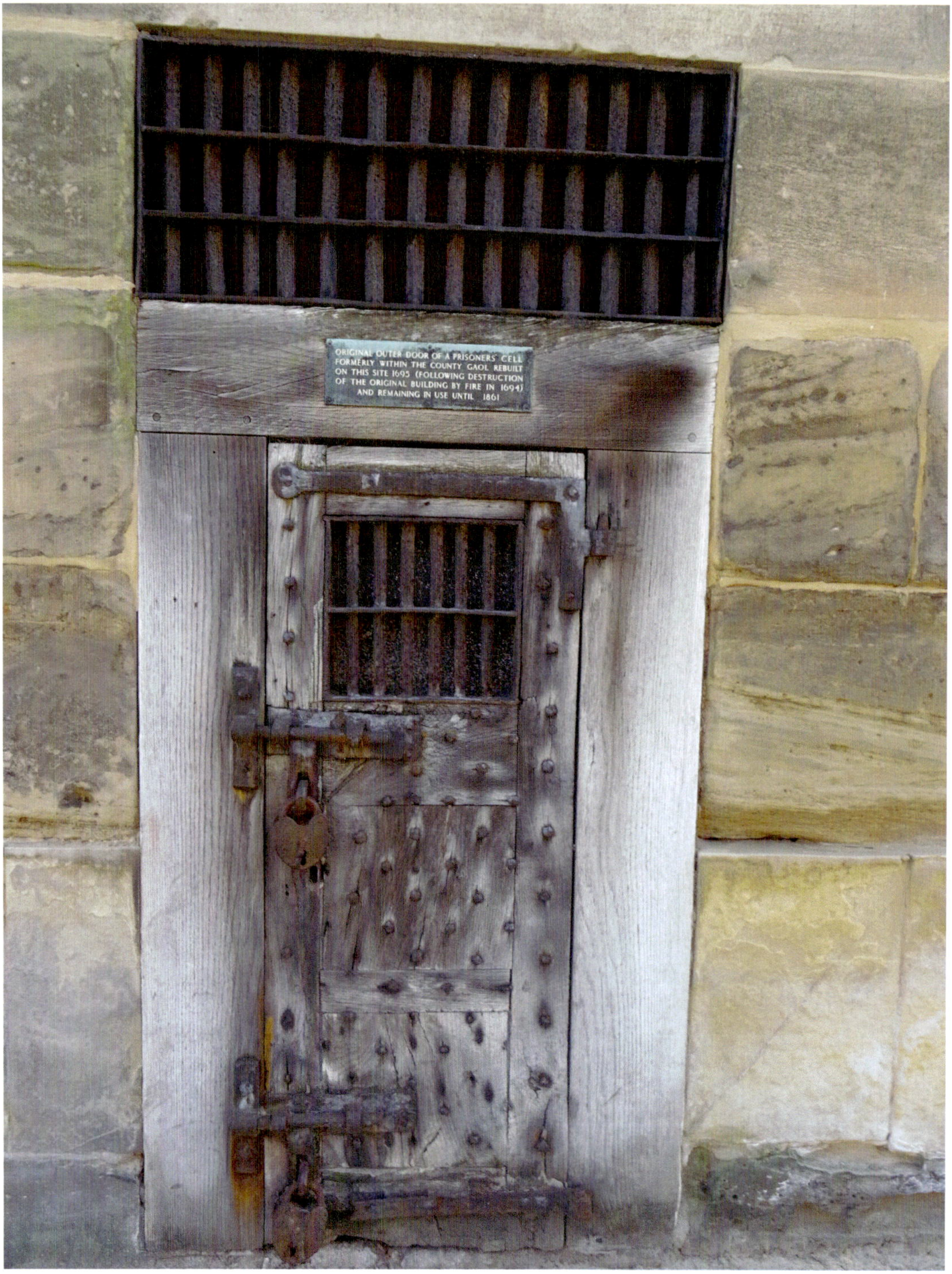

Original door to the gaol in Barrack Street. The plaque above the door reads: *Original outer door of a prisoner's cell formerly within the county gaol rebuilt on this site 1695 following destruction of the original building by fire in 1694 and remaining in use until 1861.*

The fair has its origins in the thirteenth century when the earl, John du Plessis, granted a fair for eight days when the inhabitants could erect free stalls. It was perhaps to stimulate trade that John du Plessis, soon after being granted the fair in 1261, exempted all attending it from tolls for six years and freed all but strangers from stallage. Slowness in trade at that time was probably exacerbated by merchants and tradesmen staying away from fairs because of the tolls. In 1268 tolls were worth £20 and stallage £1 10s. Fairs provided significantly for the earls' income which is why Richard Beauchamp had the date of the Michaelmas fair moved to another date in 1413. He had reported that it made no profit because six or seven other fairs in the neighbourhood were being held at the same time.

Annual fairs were significant events that attracted traders and visitors from surrounding areas. These often included livestock sales as well as stalls selling goods like cloth, iron and brass. Markets and fairs were not only economic hubs but also social gatherings where people from different walks of life could meet and interact.

Fairs and markets presented a problem for the Borough Council owing to stench, contamination and disease being spread by livestock. Sheep were removed from Sheep Street (Northgate Street) on the insistence of the justices and were confined to Brook Street, as was horses and cattle previously located in West Street, Horse Cheaping (New Street) and Rother Cheaping in Cow Lane (Brook Street).

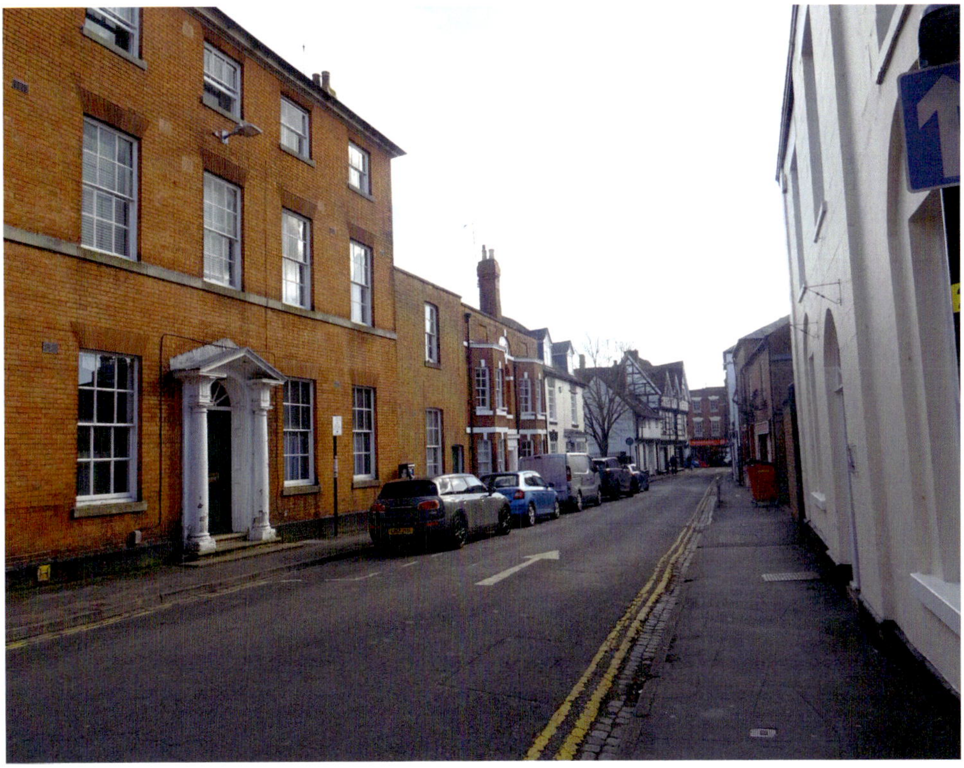

New Street (Horse Cheaping), former site of livestock sales. Horses were later removed to Brook Street (Rother Cheaping, Cow Lane).

Cattle and horses were also kept on St Mary's lands. The right to graze a horse and cow was allocated to the owners of certain houses in the parish by 1698. Their rights were ensured by customs that governed the division of tenements, which frequently occurred during rebuilding after the Great Fire. These saw that they didn't exceed the original number of commoners, given as 329 according to the 1755 Commoner's Roll. Other customs forbade 'mangy or evil diseased beasts and unshod horses'. A herdsman was employed by the chamberlains, elected by the Court Leet, to supervise the movement of cattle (drives) and mend fences.

The most significant factor in the social life of Warwick was its position as the centre of county administration. The Assizes and Quarter Sessions and the presence of the militia brought prestige to the town. Attending the Assizes were gentry, lawyers and officials and in recognition of the value placed on their attendances, sessions dinners were held and presents given to the justices. One of the aims of the Act for rebuilding the town after the Great Fire was to encourage the gentry and professional men to settle in Warwick.

This influx was at first limited to the duration of court days. Inns such as the Swan in High Street, kept by Amilion Holbeche, catered for these gentlemen. Increasingly the professional classes made their mark in the town, a result of Warwick's position as the administrative centre of the shire. The medical profession was also well represented in the town, the most notable being James Cooke of Jury Street. He was surgeon to important

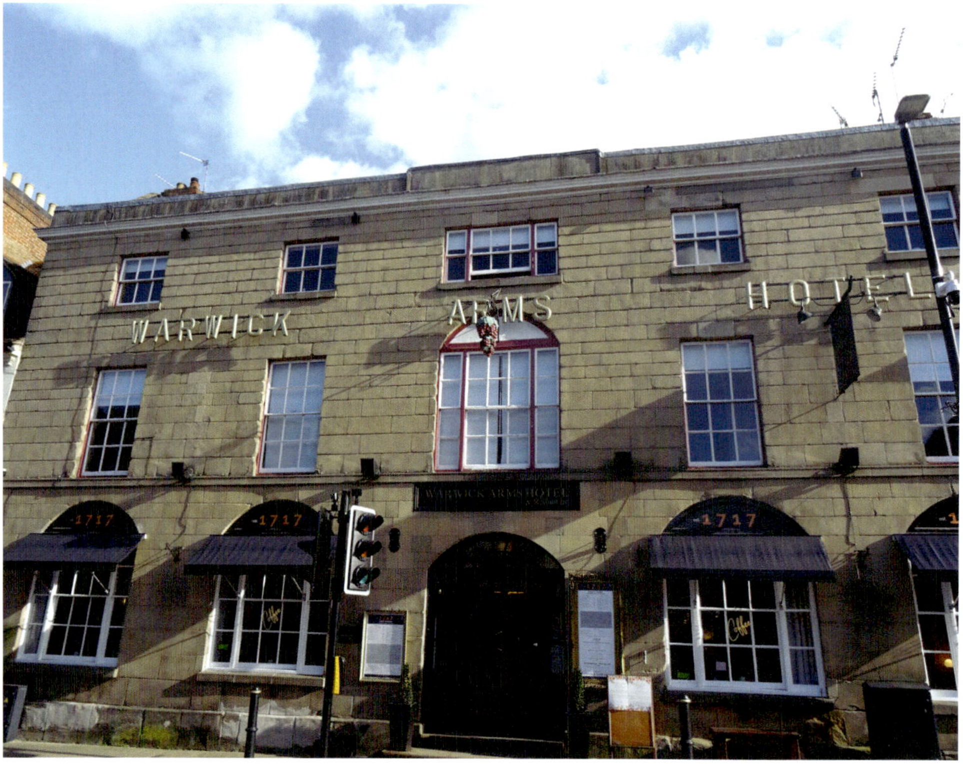

The Warwick Arms Hotel, formerly The Swan, was kept by Amilion Holbeche and catered for the influx of gentlemen attending the Assizes and Quarter Sessions in the nineteenth century.

families such as the Archers and the Brookes. It wasn't until the eighteenth century that the gentry come to reside in Warwick in any numbers.

The most notable families had their principal homes within the borough boundary. These were the Grevilles at the castle, the Puckerings at the Priory and the Stoughtons at St John's. Only the Archers of Umberslade, a very wealthy and influential family, and the Wagstaffes of Tachbrook of the important local families had town houses by the middle of the 1700s.

The Priory was one of the properties owned by Sir John Puckering, Speaker of the House of Commons and Lord Keeper of the Great Seal, who had accrued estates in Hertfordshire, Kent, Warwickshire and Lincolnshire. On his death in 1596 Puckering's wardship was sold to his widow, Lady Jane, who settled in the former Priory of St Sepulchre. The Priory was later to have a tenuous relationship with the United States.

Originally established by Henry de Newburgh in 1109, and occupied by Elizabethan Thomas Hawkins, alias Fisher, the Priory was confiscated by Henry VIII in 1536. The monastic buildings of St Sepulchre's Priory were demolished by Thomas Hawkins who built a new house called The Priory in 1566. Sir John Puckering came into possession in 1581, and it was acquired by Henry Wise in 1709 whose family retained ownership until 1851. The Priory descended by marriage to Sir Wathen Waller and was abandoned in 1809. It was later sold to the Oxford Junction Railway Company. The shell of the house was purchased by the Borough Council in 1925 and advertised for sale, which met with a great deal of local opposition.

Despite opposition, the sale went ahead and it was purchased by American Alexander Weddell, the United States Ambassador to Spain, who had it dismantled. The stones were numbered and shipped to America where they were re-erected in Richmond, Virginia, although not a faithful copy of the original building. Following the deaths of Mr Weddell and his wife, in a train crash in 1948, the building Virginia House was deeded to the Virginia Historical Society.

Priory Park estate remained in the hands of the Wise and Waller families after the sale of the Priory. This area included Priory Pools, originally fishponds belonging to the former monastery of St Sepulchre. These were later filled in and levelled in 1965 to provide an extension to Priory Park. Priory Park was to provide the venue for the International Scouts Jamboree (Amikaro) in 1979 when scouts from nine countries came to Warwick.

Continuing influx of gentry into the town throughout the eighteenth century was reflected in the development of a 'Gentleman's Party' in the 1760s, which was an important factor in town politics until the turn of the century. This saw an increase in the castle influence over the Corporation. In 1759 the earl had refused to entertain any idea of supporting the Corporation, being comprised of shopkeepers and craftsmen who had been members ever since the borough was first incorporated. The development of the 'Gentleman's Party' incorporated new members of the Corporation. These were professional men, although not necessarily castle nominees, and was to retain the influence of the earl which had a significant effect on the course of the borough history.

A new social order also required fashionable entertainments with the most prominent being the introduction of the races. Warwick was also blessed with open commonable land. This was further extended to the west in the latter half of the thirteenth century by

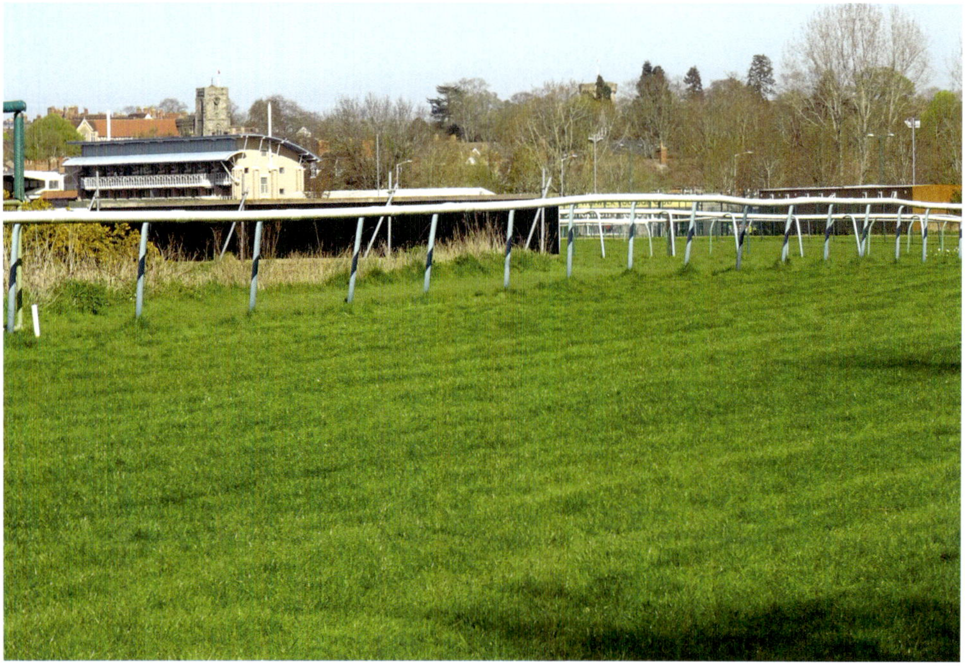

The racecourse. Races were established in 1707 by Lord Brooke who gave £15. to the Chamberlains to make a horse race.

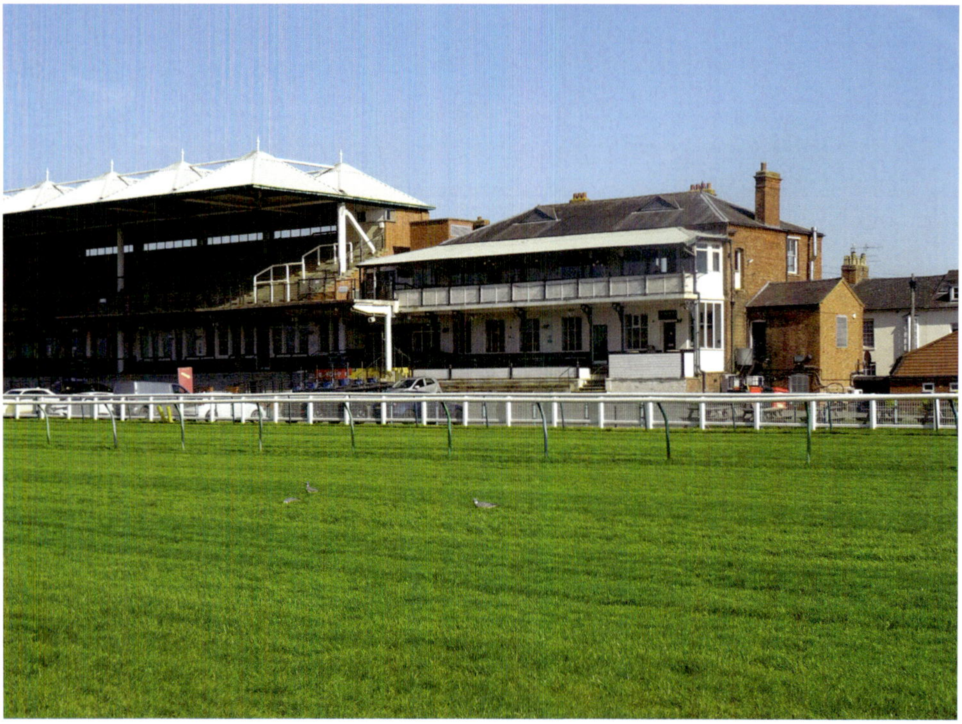

Grandstands on the racecourse. The first grandstand was erected in 1802.

a gift of land by Margery, widow of Earl John du Plessis and was to enable horse-racing to take place in the eighteenth century. In 1707 Lord Brooke gave £15. to the Chamberlains to make a horse-race. By 1775 the races, then held in September, provided entertainment on two days. On each evening balls were held in the Shire Hall and public breakfasts were staged at the Court House. The sport was to grow in popularity and a grandstand was erected in 1802. Races and fairs encouraged beggars, who were a nuisance in the town.

Theatrical entertainments were provided in the town during race meetings and occasionally at other times. A theatre had been built by 1792 and John Boles Watson of the Theatre Royal, Cheltenham, also planned to erect a new theatre in the Market Place. He proposed to open it for 'dramas' on race and other public days. This does not appear to have found favour with the inhabitants of the Market Place who objected to this plan and Watson was forced to return to his 'old shop', the theatre in Cocksparrow Hall (Theatre Street). Roger Kemble, a strolling player, was later to own the theatre and his daughter, Sarah, who became the famous Shakespearean actress Sarah Siddons, also performed there.

The social round for the townspeople was completed with attractions such as race balls, hunt balls, concerts, winter assemblies and card parties, usually held at the Court House. These not only catered for the townspeople but for those who came to the area drawn by the fame of the castle and later by the medicinal springs of nearby Leamington.

Throughout the shifting fortunes of the inhabitants of the castle, it was perhaps George Guy Greville, 4th Earl of Warwick who was to experience a great change in his personal circumstances. This was precipitated by a fire in 1871. The fire, which broke out in Lady Warwick's dressing room, quickly took hold and spread to the east wing, enveloping the Great Hall and private apartments.

The Great Hall was gutted but due to a fire gap in the roof cut by firemen, the flames were checked before they could reach the State Rooms. The two Greville children with their nurse managed to make their way down the winding stairs to the grand staircase before it was engulfed in flames. The Reverend V. R. Smythe, vicar of St Nicholas Church, then took them to the Warwick Arms Hotel. Most of the treasures such as pictures and books were saved, the serious losses being in the Great Hall where an antique marble bust of Hercules, armour and a Greek sarcophagus were destroyed.

Earl George Greville was distraught as his financial situation meant that he didn't have the funds to restore his home. The local tradesmen were also disconcerted as they saw their livelihoods being adversely affected with the tourist trade dropping off. Warwick Castle was first exploited as a tourist attraction in 1816 and in 1825–26 there were as many as 6,000 visitors that year. To forestall this, the tradesmen started a public restoration fund which eventually reached £9,651, and the work to restore the castle to its former glory was commenced.

George Greville commissioned Anthony Salvin to do the restoration. He was an architect of some repute whose works included, among others, work on Windsor Castle, Rockingham Castle and the Tower of London. As the restoration was publicly funded, this saw the status of the castle effectively changed from being a home to that of a business. This situation did not suit the earl, but he had no choice other than to accept that through public contribution to its restoration, the castle had now come to be seen as the people's

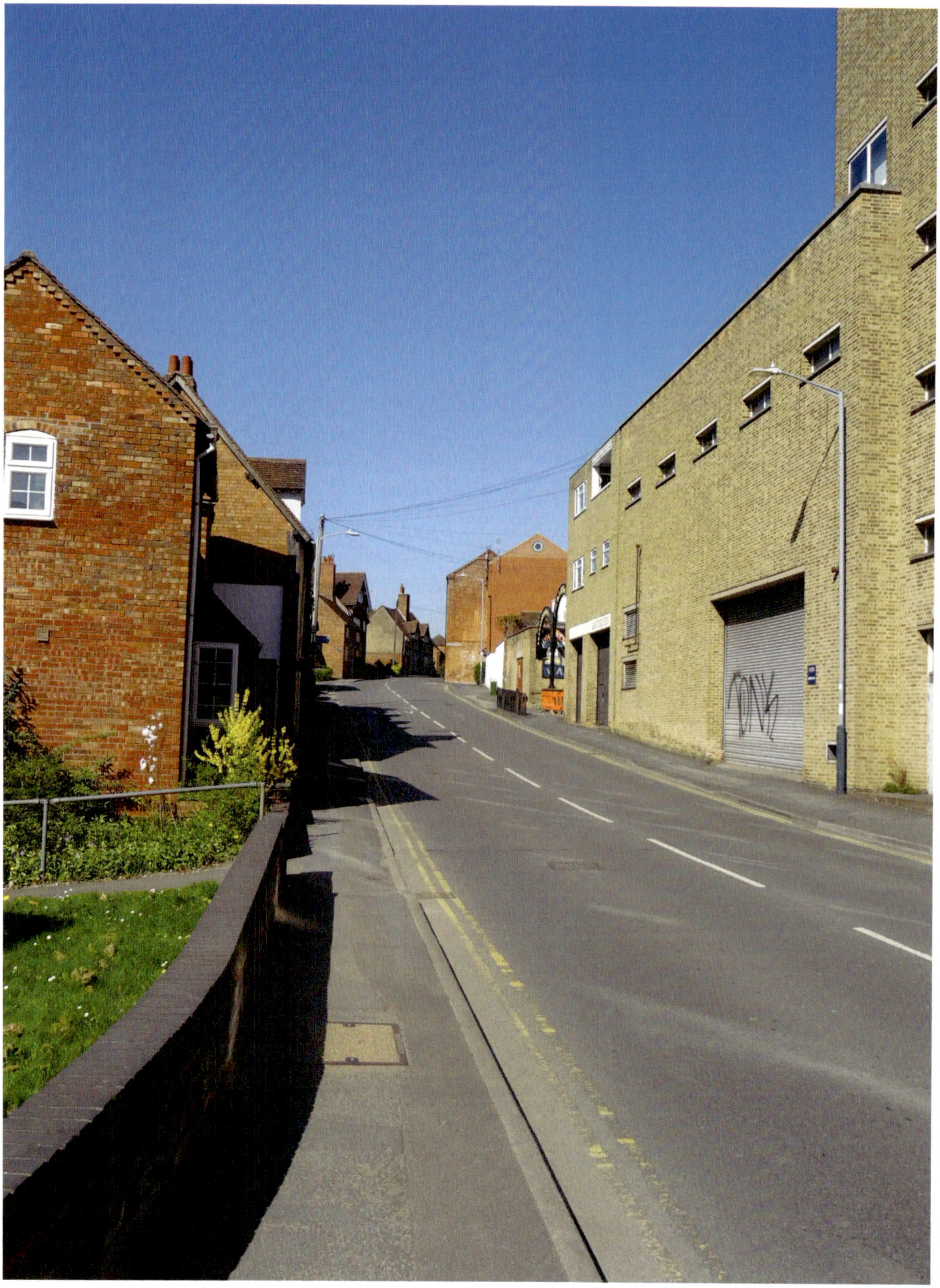

Theatre Street, site of the theatre in 1792 that was demolished in the mid-nineteenth century and replaced with a slaughterhouse.

property. About this time there was a growing Social Democrat movement which was in favour of placing the national treasures such as stately homes in public ownership, giving the people access to them.

By 1885 visitors to the castle must have presented something of a nuisance to the earl as he closed the castle. This caused much consternation in the town, and it was reported that eight Americans who were staying in one of the principal hotels left hurriedly. They had cited inability to gain access to the castle as their reason for departure. The castle was reopened shortly afterwards.

In his later years, George Greville was to witness a scandal that rocked Warwick and Leamington and reverberated throughout Warwickshire and beyond. It was said to rival the disaster of the Great Fire. This was the failure of the bank of Greenway, Smith & Greenway in 1887, causing a great deal of distress and hardship. The bank had been established for a hundred years. Unwise investments had led to bankruptcy and owing creditors £275,000. Misappropriation of funds saw Mr G. C. Greenway sentenced to five years' penal servitude and Mr Kelynge Greenway to one year's hard labour.

George Greville was a Tory Member of Parliament for South Warwickshire from 1845–53 and died in 1893. He was buried at St Mary's.

The *Victoria County History - Vol. 8* records that the rapid increase in population in the first three decades of the nineteenth century, particularly among the labouring and artisan classes, had a considerable effect on the social as well as the political sphere. The influx of Irish labourers employed to build the canals and whose votes were so eagerly canvassed in the alehouses and the appearance of small shopkeepers in the town in increasing numbers created new problems for public administration. Initially these were tackled on a voluntary basis by the establishment of a Watch Committee in 1819 'for preventing a continuance of nightly depredations on their property'.

To address the problem of public health, the Corporation was urged to endorse byelaws to regulate the emptying of privies. They were also called upon to prevent such nuisances as wheeling barrows and rolling lead on the flagging and to discourage loiterers and idlers on street corners at night 'to the annoyance and frequent insult of females'. The Leet Jury drew attention to the need for paved crossings at various places in the town and suggested that the poor from the workhouse could be employed scraping the roads and sweeping the crossings in winter.

Contributing to the rapid increase in the town's population in the early part of the nineteenth century was the influx of immigrants. In the thirty years from 1801–31 the population increased from 3,592 to 9,109. An upsurge in manufacturing during the Napoleonic Wars called for more labour. Other industry was the paving and flagging of the streets in 1810, and in 1822 the gasworks was opened. A tramway joining the gasworks to the Great Western Railway across the Pigwells was constructed and used between 1828 and 1905.

Increasing economic activity in the town and corporation attention to public welfare had brought improvements by 1815. The water supply for parts of the town had been improved and shopfronts were 'newly fronted and fitted up'. The whole presented Warwick as a neat, airy, spacious, handsome and flourishing town. In 1830 the market was said to be constantly improving with highly respectable businesses – that is drapers, other shops and first-class inns. The rapidly increasing trade at this time was probably accounted for by Warwick's proximity to the fashionable spa town of Leamington. The growth of Leamington Spa was purported to be an increasingly important factor in the growth of the town.

A flourishing town needed links with other towns and cities and communications by coach were established with Birmingham, Coventry, Leicester, Gloucester, Bristol and London. By 1830 there were fourteen coach routes through Warwick with nine daily connecting with London, Liverpool, Wolverhampton, Oxford and Cheltenham.

Coaches were to be ousted by the provision of a railway service. In 1844 John Molladay, hatter, led a move in favour of railways. He had objected to Warwick being treated as a village and stressed the acute need for a link to the railway centre in Rugby. Links were established and in 1850 trains provided a daily service to Cheltenham, Oxford, Stratford-upon-Avon and Alcester, with less frequent services to Henley-in-Arden, Shipston-on-Stour and Worcester. All coach services had ceased by 1874. Omnibuses from the 'Warwick Arms' and 'Woolpack' met all trains arriving at Warwick and Milverton stations.

Other forms of transport were the introduction of horse-drawn trams in 1881. These ran from High Street, through Smith Street, Coten-End and Milverton to Leamington. Electric trams superseded the horse-drawn trams in 1905.

The need to house the immigrants, many unskilled labourers, led to the layout of new streets and a growth of working-class quarters to the west and north-west of the old town. The cramped nature of these housing areas may have been influenced by the shortage of suitable sites close to the town because of large areas of common lands and private parks that surrounded it. The town's shopkeepers profited by the increase in this industrial activity. Part of their additional trade was fostered by the development of nearby Leamington as a fashionable spa, since many people came into Warwick to buy before good shops were built in Leamington itself.

Large-scale building works meant that dreadful living conditions existed alongside elegance. The new working-class houses and cramped, insanitary courts and tenements were constructed behind existing houses and approached through alleys. The water supply was bad. Sewage flowed into a withy bed between the castle and the bridge.

The *Warwick Advertiser* reported in 1849 that there were between 200 and 300 folks in forty-two houses with eight pigsties, a couple of pumps and just two privies. These were the Brookhouse or Commercial buildings erected on the Birmingham Road *c.* 1813 with thirty-six back-to-back houses together with the Dun Cow Inn. The dwellings were strongly condemned by the Inspector of Health in 1849. Brookhouse buildings were to be superseded by a small development called Saltisford Gardens in 1962.

The *Victoria County History - Vol 8* states that a report by a Public Health Inspector published in 1849 drew attention to the stark reality that bad drainage, overcrowding and poor water supplies were demonstrated to be the source of an increasing mortality rate which had risen considerably in the previous two years. Water obtained from the Priory Pools and the river was described as very hard and often impure. Streets in the centre of town were said to be in 'moderate' condition, most footways were flagged and some carriageways were pitched or macadamized. There were six surveyors of highways in the

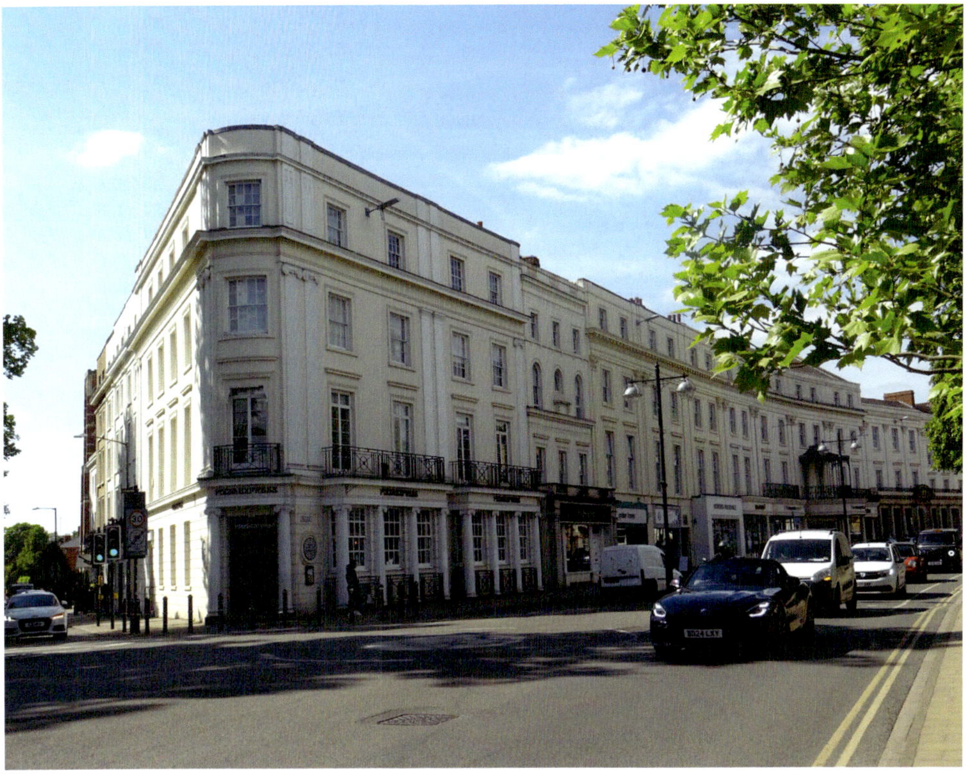

The fashionable spa town of Leamington attracted visitors who then went to Warwick to visit the castle and shop, boosting trade.

town 'not acting in concert and working upon no fixed system'. The work was thought to be badly and probably expensively done.

A need to cater for the sick was provided for by the Warwick Dispensary for the sick and poor, founded in 1826. This was aided by public subscriptions and the Warwick Provident Sick Association founded in 1857 by the vicar of St Paul's. These amalgamated in 1871 to form the Warwick Dispensary which provided a limited number of beds in the Castle Street premises. The service ceased on the introduction of the National Health Service in 1948.

Provision also had to be made for the poor, needy, unemployed, elderly and infirm. A new Warwick Union workhouse was erected in 1837–9 on the east side of what became known as Union Road (Lakin Road). Designed by W. Watson, architect, on the cruciform layout, separate male and female accommodation was placed on either side of the central block containing a boardroom, administration offices and Master's quarters. Visiting the workhouse in 1895, Edward, Prince of Wales wrote in the visitor's book: 'I have visited this Union with great interest and have found everything very clean, the inmates well cared for and everything in excellent order.' Perhaps we should expect nothing less on the visit of royalty.

Political and social unrest followed an election in 1832 after the passing of the Reform Bill. This disenfranchised fifty-six boroughs in England and Wales and reduced another

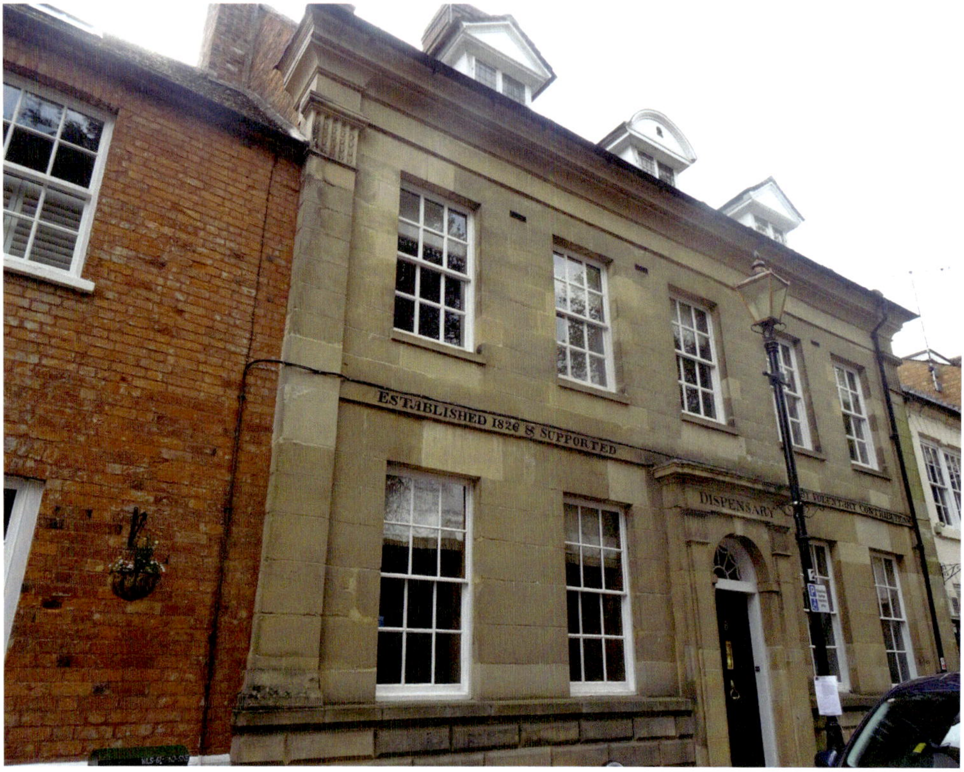

Warwick Dispensary. Once used for treating the sick, it became redundant with the commencement of the National Health Service in 1948.

thirty-one to only one MP. As well as getting rid of the Rotten Boroughs, the Reform Bill also formalised the exclusion of women from voting in Parliamentary elections. The property qualifications also meant most working men still could not vote. This led to widespread discontent and Whigs and Tories clashed violently in Warwick. Rioting ensued and men were badly injured. All the windows in the George Inn in the Market Place were smashed. The Scots Greys who were based in the town were obliged to tackle the mob and remove them from the streets.

John Tomes, an attorney who had taken a house in Jury Street, Warwick, in 1783 had established himself among the leaders of the Warwick Reform or Independent Party. In 1792 he was the agent for Robert Knight, the challenger to Lord Warwick's Castle interest. As a political reformer, Tomes had commenced canvassing at the General Election Reform dinner in 1832, making his long residence and support for retrenchment, reform and the abolition of slavery the cornerstone of his campaign. Dismayed to be defeated at the General Election through in his view the chicanery of the Earl of Warwick, he did not stand for Parliament again. The earl was not above bribing others, as demonstrated by the 1833 election enquiry. This named twenty-six alehouses as having been implicated in the Greville interest. These were paid by the earl to dispense hospitality on behalf of the Tory candidate.

The political scene was still volatile when the threat of violence reared its head again in Warwick in 1848. The working classes had declared themselves to be Chartists at crowded meetings throughout the country in March. Their political aims were universal suffrage. These were viewed with concern by the authorities and some of the propertied classes had come to believe that the Chartist movement was intent on a revolution. As a precaution, muskets and pistols from the Tower of London were issued to the 'Brethren' at the Lord Leycester Hospital during the Chartist trouble.

A passionate advocate of the Chartist movement, John Collins and fellow 'moral force' Chartist William Lovett were arrested on charges of sedition (rebellious conduct and writings) and sentenced to twelve months in Warwick gaol. Their mistreatment in gaol was the subject of much debate in Parliament and newspapers nationwide. While in prison they wrote a book entitled *Chartism: A New Organisation of the People*. The emphasis was on education and called for such things as public schools and libraries as well as for clean, wholesome living.

Warwick did provide for education initially for boys only. The imposing building of St John's House, formerly the Hospital of St John the Baptist in Henry II's reign, and a victim of Henry VIII's Dissolution of the Monasteries, was rebuilt by Nathaniel Stoughton between 1666 and 1670. This was to serve as a private school in 1791 and a prospectus offered education for 'young gentlemen, who are genteelly boarded, tenderly and affectionately treated, liberally educated and moderately charged'.

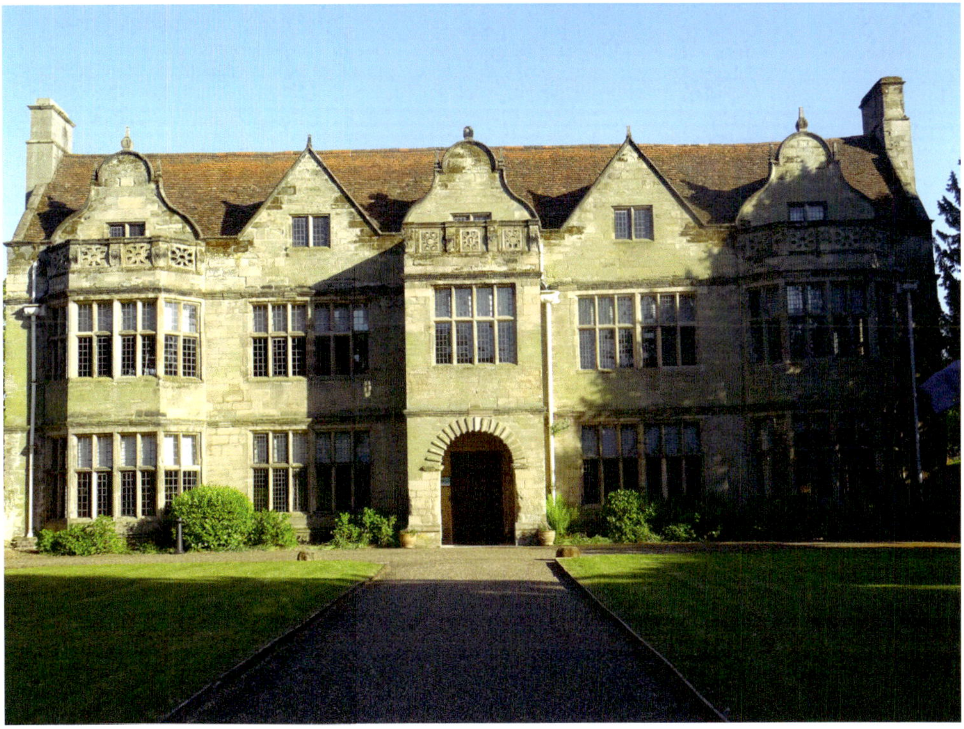

St John's House was rebuilt by Nathaniel Stoughton between 1666 and 1670. This served as a private school in 1791 and later a military pay record office.

Most children not privately educated were taught in 1851 in schools conducted by the two national societies. The National Society appears to have begun work in Warwick in 1815 when classes attended by twenty-seven pupils were held at the gaol. In 1849 ninety-one children attended classes in Warwick Union Workhouse, originally established in St Mary's parish workhouse in the Saltisford. The Wesleyan Chapel, built in 1834 in Chapel Street, reopened in 1835 as a boys' school with 150 pupils. This was known as the Borough School. Education was free until 1847 when a weekly fee of 1d per child began to be charged.

At the time of the education census of 1851, 1,461 children attended day schools in Warwick. These comprised of thirty-four private schools and nine public schools, the oldest being the King's Grammar School. This was based in St John's Church in the Market Place in the latter fifteenth century and the Lord Leycester Hospital from 1546–71, endowed as a grammar school by Henry VIII. The school was reputed to have its origins in the time of Edward the Confessor in 1042–66. It later relocated to St Peter's Chapel over Eastgate. Between the late seventeenth century and 1849 the King's School, as it was then known, was situated in the College of the Vicar's Choral in St Mary's churchyard. Following a merger with the King's Middle School in the Butts, it became Warwick School. The school relocated to a new building on the Myton Road designed by J. Cundall in 1849.

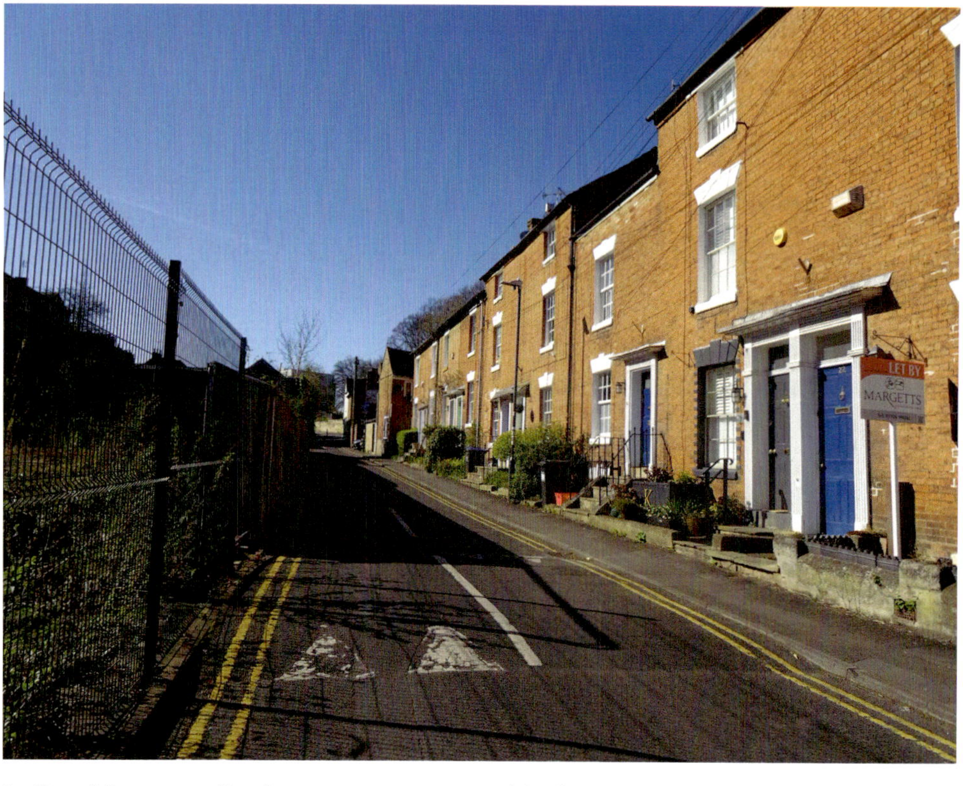

In Chapel Street a medieval quarry pit, a seventeenth/eighteenth-century stone vaulted cellar and well were revealed at Nos 9–11 during observation.

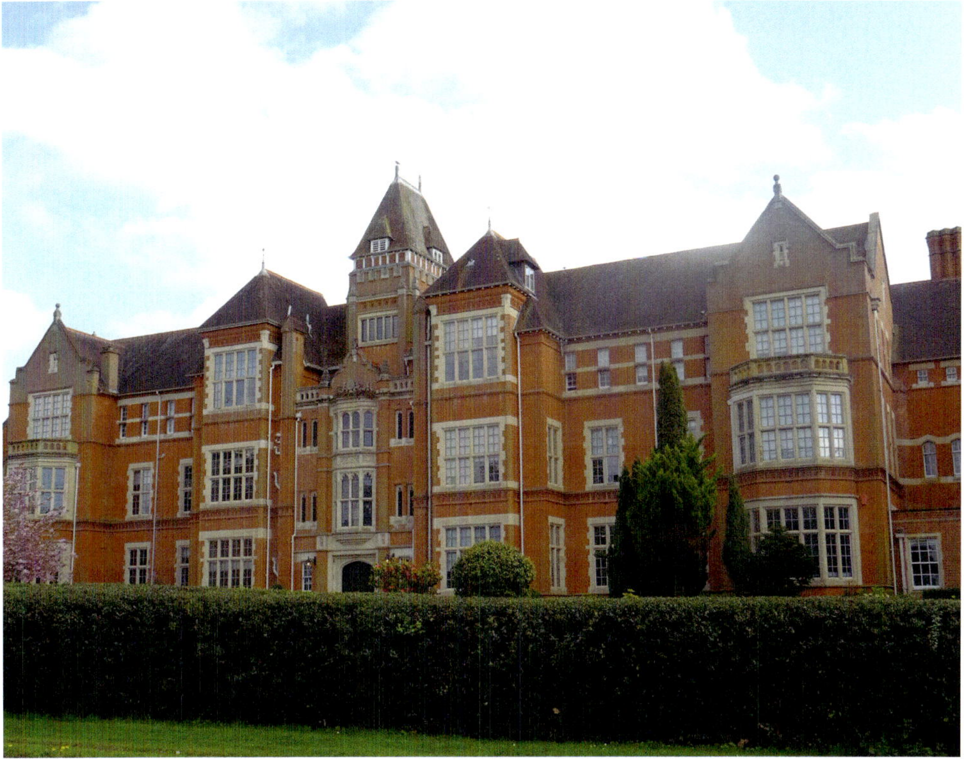

Warwick School, designed by J. Cundall, 1849.

A Charity School, Castle Street School of Industry for Girls was established around 1790 by the Countess of Warwick. The school occupied Thomas Oken's house from 1809–23. In 1833 this depended entirely on subscriptions and was said to be chiefly supported by the Greville family and the Reverend Henry Wise.

Sunday schools were also instrumental in the education of children. One of the first achievements of Unitarian William Field who came to Warwick in 1789 was to build a Sunday school where poor children could be taught to read and write. This however was to become controversial. Under Field's influence the Warwick Unitarians played a leading part in the local agitation for parliamentary reform. The beginning of his ministry coincided with the outbreak of the French Revolution, the first effect of which in England was to revive the antagonism of the church towards dissenters (Nonconformists) after nearly a century, culminating in the Birmingham Riots (Priestley Riots) of July 1791. These had repercussions in Warwick which saw a hot dispute over Sunday schools in which Anglicans accused the Unitarians of using their school to undermine the established church and demanded that it be closed.

School attendances declined steadily in the 1900s apart from a temporary increase after the First World War following an increase in birth rates. This was due to Warwick's population having become middle-aged by that time.

Clubs and societies were to mushroom in the nineteenth century to cater for the intellectual and recreational tastes of the inhabitants. In *Warwick in Times Past*

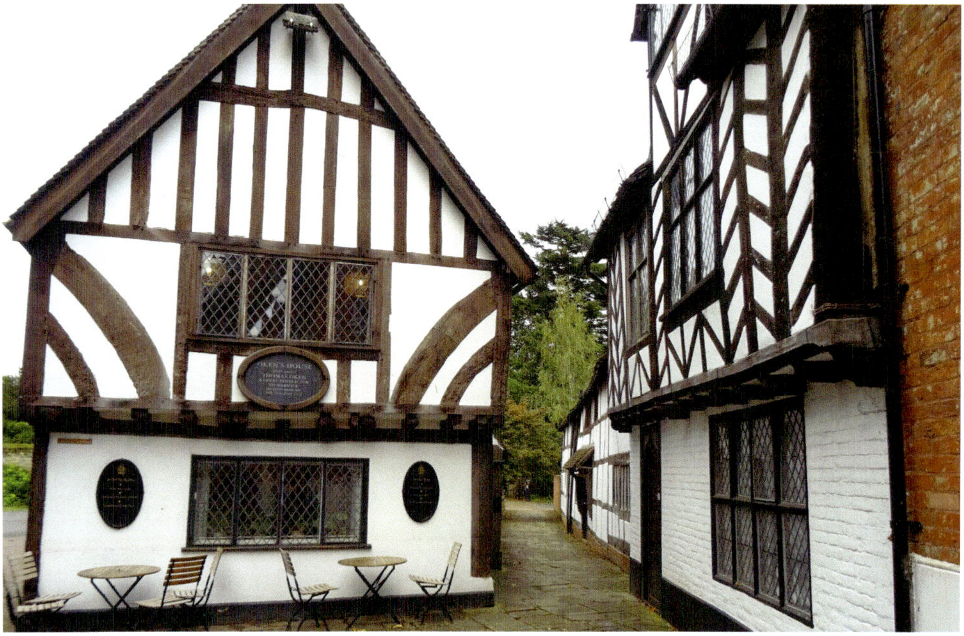

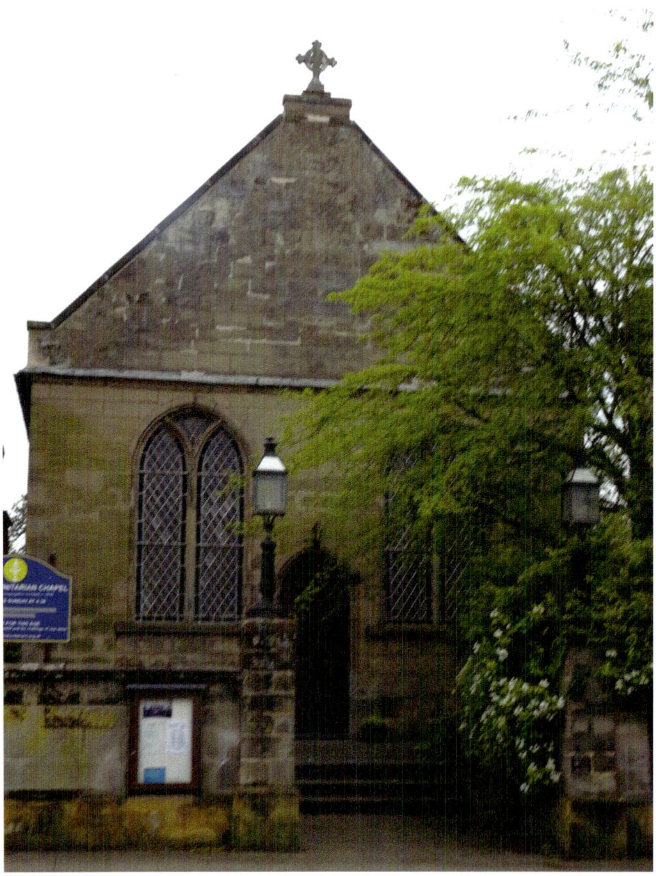

Above: Thomas Oken's House. The Castle Street School of Industry for Girls was located here, established in 1790 by the Countess of Warwick.

Left: Unitarian Chapel, High Street, built in 1780, was established as a Sunday school for poor children to learn to read and write by Unitarian William Field in 1789.

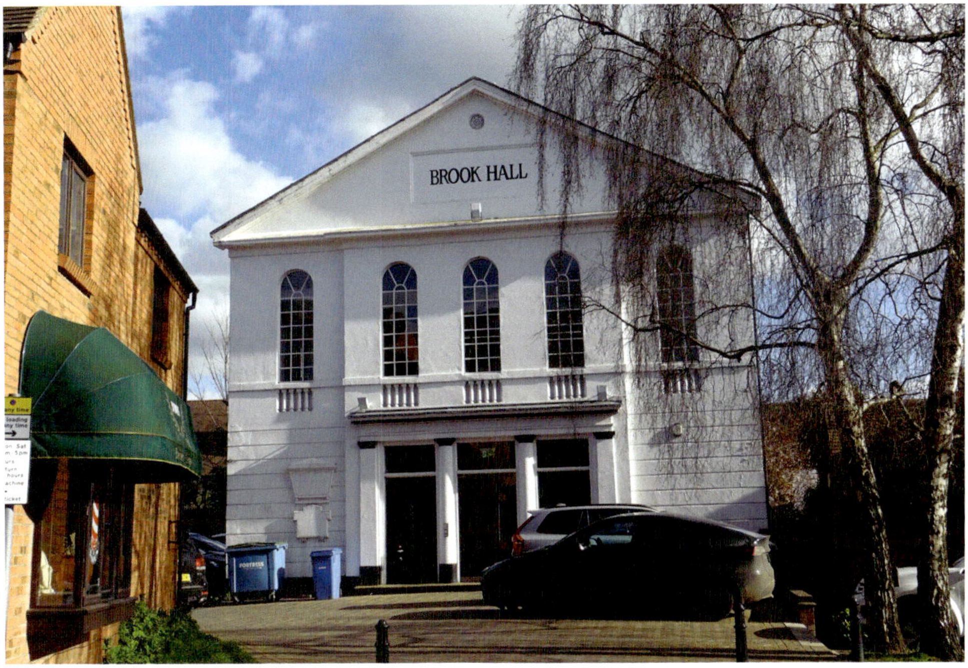

Brook Street Congregational Church. The Nonconformist church was first established in the mid-eighteenth century and replaced with a larger building in 1826. It closed in 1981.

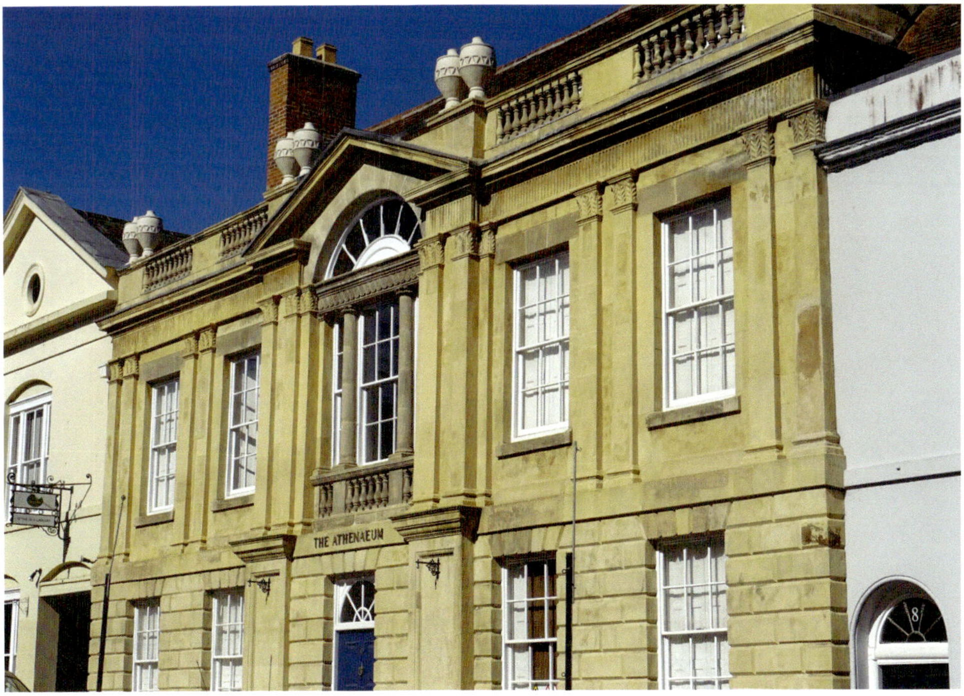

Athenaeum, Church Street, providing a reading room and library for intellectual and moral pursuits in 1846.

P. J. E. Gates records that facilities for moral and intellectual development were catered for by the aid of a library, reading and newsroom provided by the Athenaeum in Church Street which opened in 1846.

In 1836 the Warwickshire Natural History and Archaeological Society was formed and established a museum in the Market Hall. Through field collecting and gifts from individuals, the society's collection grew quickly. More display space was needed and by 1840 the whole top part of the Market Hall was in use. The society particularly flourished under the influence of the eminent geologist the Reverend Peter Brodie. The museum declined in the 1880s due to financial difficulties and lack of public support but was saved by the efforts of William Gibbins, a local landowner and Quaker, from the late nineteenth century. Other intellectual pursuits were the creation in 1837 of the Warwickshire Institute for Readings and Lectures.

On the sporting scene the Warwick Old Cricket Club was founded in 1841 and polo was regularly played on St Mary's Common by 1885. A golf club was established on Warwick Common in 1886.

Not only did clubs, societies and entertainments provide for the amusement of the populace, but on occasion the visit of royalty to the castle was greeted with a certain degree of excitement and anticipation. The *Warwick Advertiser* reported that in 1839 Queen Adelaide, widow of William IV, visited Warwick. She was escorted by the Earl of Aylesford's troop of the Warwickshire Yeomanry Cavalry through Coventry and Kenilworth and conducted to Guy's Cliffe by Lord Leigh where she was met by numerous carriages of the nobility and gentry. The cavalcade then proceeded to the town and castle where the Earl, Henry Richard Greville, was waiting to greet her.

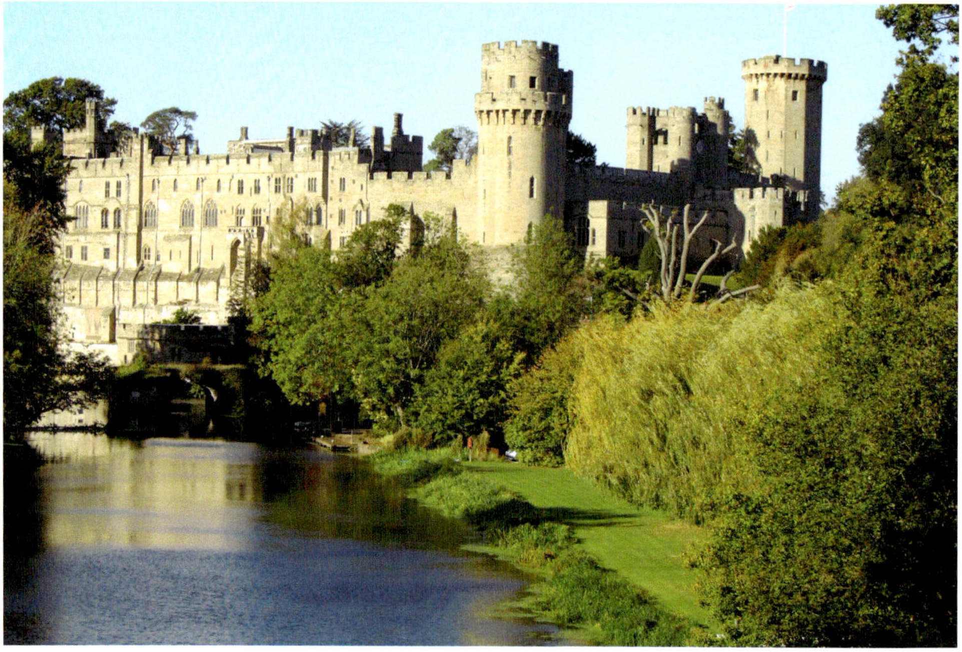

Warwick Castle. Queen Adelaide, widow of William IV, was entertained here in 1839.

Queen Adelaide was welcomed by a triumphal arch, crowds in carriages, on horseback and foot, with thirty waggons drawn up in line accommodating wildly cheering schoolchildren. As a parting gift, the dowager Queen gave fifty pounds to the Reverend John Boudier for the purpose of providing warm winter cloaks for a number of 'needy old ladies'.

Queen Victoria and Prince Albert made a brief visit to the castle in June 1858 amid much pomp and ceremony after visiting nearby Stoneleigh Abbey and opening the Aston Hall, which no doubt increased its popularity as a tourist attraction. Following luncheon in the banqueting hall, the royal couple paraded around the grounds and viewed the recently erected additions to the castle. Prince Albert also climbed Guy's Tower. After viewing the famous Warwick Vase in the conservatory, the royal party proceeded to the riverbank where the Queen planted an oak and Prince Albert planted a Wellingtonia. The beautiful Victorian rose garden which later was allowed to deteriorate was recreated and opened by Lady Diana, Princess of Wales in 1982.

The visits of the Prince of Wales, later Edward VII, to the castle were rather more discreet. These were leaked by Lord Warwick's servants and he was reported to have been much irritated by sightseers. His affair with the Countess Frances Evelyn Maynard (Daisy) was perhaps just a matter of speculation at that time. The Countess, or 'Daisy', was a flamboyant and generous woman well known to the people of Warwick for her habit of flinging half-crowns out of the motorcar when she passed through the town.

A wealthy heiress upon inheriting the family fortune, Frances was to spend lavishly on designer dresses, parties and entertaining. The most prolific of all was the 'Bal Poudre' where 400 guests were asked to dress in the costumes of Louis XIV and XVI complete with powdered wigs. The Countess made her appearance as Marie Antoinette.

The marriage of Lord Francis Guy Greville to Frances Evelyn Maynard in 1881 marked the beginning of a turbulent relationship that saw scandal and intrigue. Frances at the age of twenty-eight was to embark on a nine-year affair with Edward, Prince of Wales. She became a member of the exclusive Marlborough House Set, in which Edward was also a member. Frances later became a committed socialist – although known as a champagne socialist because of her wealth – after her encounter with Robert Blatchford, editor of *The Clarion*, and became involved in charitable works in Warwick. The countess also entertained political ambitions. She stood as the Independent Labour candidate for Warwick and Leamington in 1923 but lost to her cousin Anthony Eden who was later to become Prime Minister.

Lady Warwick's generosity also extended to providing the castle grounds as a venue for the entertainment of the townsfolk. A pageant was held in July 1906 and was described by the *Warwick Advertiser* as 'the biggest thing that had ever happened to Warwick'. The idea of a Warwick Pageant originated with Edward Hicks, journalist, and was thought so ingenious that it was taken up. The object was to tell the story of Warwick and its rise with the establishment of Ethelfleda's Mound, a defensive structure; the deeds which made it famous; the civilisation of the people, and how they gained their civic liberties and the part they played in moulding the character of the nation. It was produced by Louis N. Parker with a cast of 2,000.

Pageant week began on Sunday 1 July with a special service at St Mary's Collegiate Church, preached by the Bishop of Bristol. This was in line with Louis Parker's ideas about pageants, who was always insistent that pageant week should commence with special church services.

The antiquity of Christian belief in Warwick is highlighted in episode one where Caratacus, a first-century AD British chieftain, is shown saving a child from pagan sacrifice.

This glorious theatrical event presented a history of Warwick in twelve episodes and included a state barge for Elizabeth I on the Avon and a huge dun cow drawn into the arena with flaming eyes. The preparations were presided over by the Mayor of Warwick, Thomas Kemp. An Executive Committee was established at what was to become known as the Pageant House in Jury Street, to launch a fund based on public subscriptions and guarantees to underwrite the cost of the event. A Ladies Committee was formed and 300 ladies sewed 1,400 costumes.

Episodes included the trial of Piers Gaveston, Duke of Cornwall and a great favourite with Edward II. Other scenes included the Kingmaker taken from Shakespeare's Henry VI production. This produced the greatest feudal display of the day. As the cavalcade came slowly down the arena the Kingmaker snatched the crown from Edward's head and marched off to free Henry from imprisonment. The grand finale depicted Britannia richly arrayed in white crepe with a gold cuirass embroidered with sequins and jewels complete with a magnificent train 7 yards in length and a golden helmet sporting a royal blue feather.

Throughout, the narrative of the pageant portrayed the pivotal roles of the earls as a central theme of Warwick's history. Louis N. Parker was later to refer to Warwick as 'the Clapham Junction of English history'.

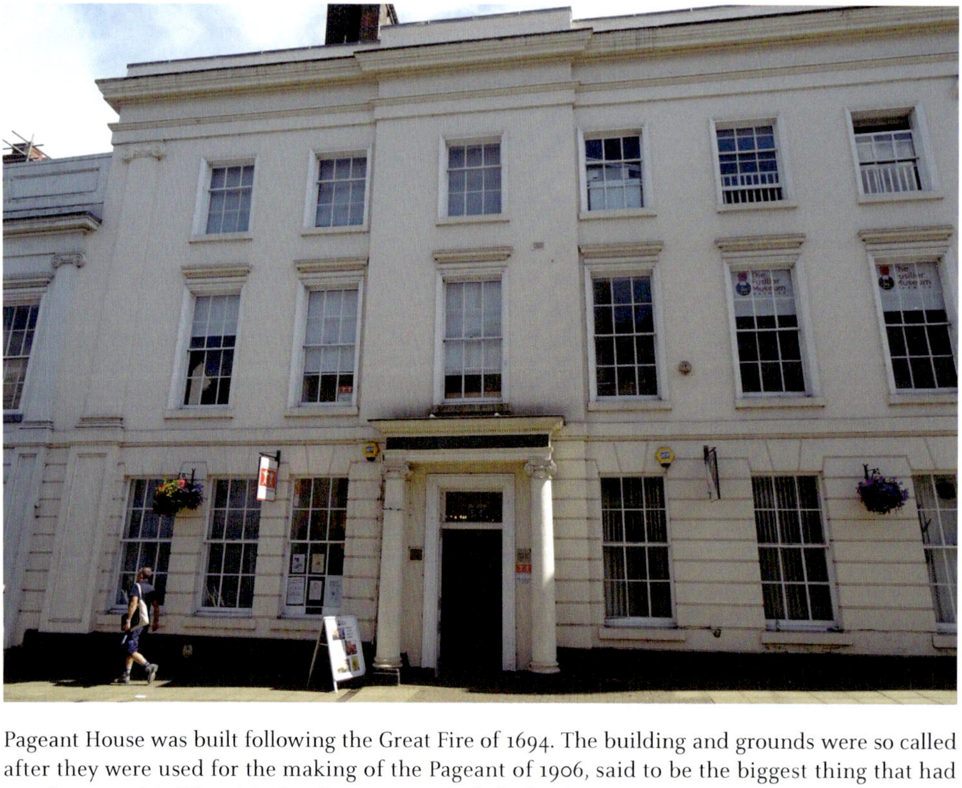

Pageant House was built following the Great Fire of 1694. The building and grounds were so called after they were used for the making of the Pageant of 1906, said to be the biggest thing that had ever happened in Warwick. Previous owners included Kelynge Greenway in 1871 and Sir Edward Montague, Mayor of Warwick.

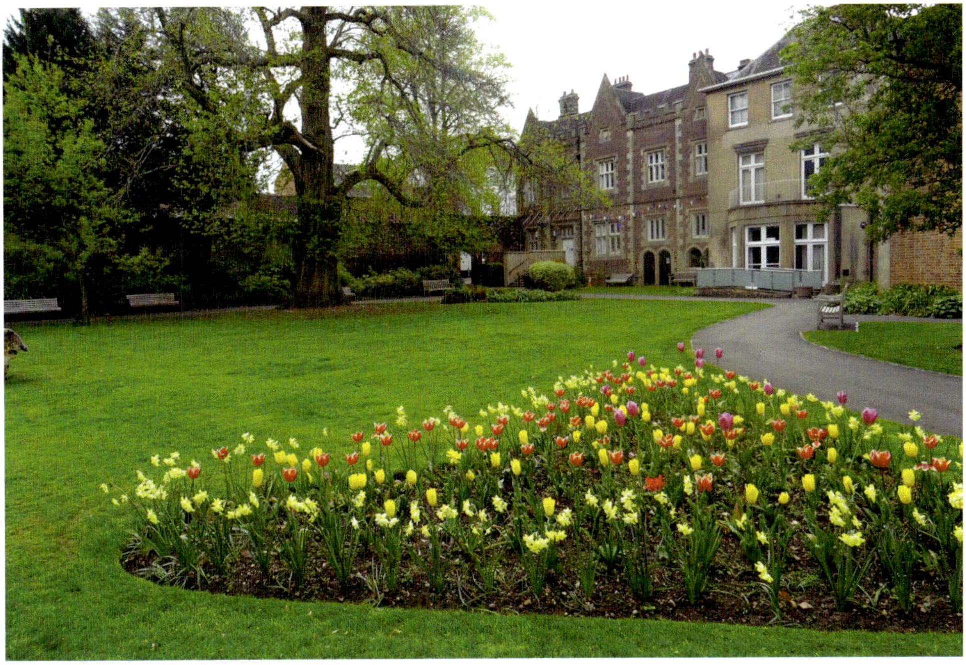

Pageant House Gardens are open to the public.

Commenting on the loan of the grounds for rehearsals and pageant, Lady Warwick said of the castle, 'It is a national glory as well as a personal possession and we who hold it now, strive to fulfil, imperfectly it may be, the duties of our stewardship and the privilege of our heritage.'

The castle grounds were again the venue for the Coronation Pageant in 1953 and featured many of the local schoolchildren. Following in the family footsteps, the producer was Anthony Parker, grandson of Louis N. Parker.

Excitement generated by the pageant, which had attracted people from all over the world, thereby extending Warwick's standing and prominence as a county town, was replaced with more sombre feelings eight years later with the outbreak of the First World War in 1914. The Royal Warwickshire Regiment and Warwickshire Yeomanry were called up and trained and camped on St Mary's Lands. Also assigned to the Royal Warwickshire Regiment was Bernard Montgomery, commissioned as a second lieutenant and based at Budbrooke Barracks. Brooke's Battery of the 1st Warwickshire Royal Horse Artillery, first raised in 1908 with volunteer soldiers, saw the most action in 1916–18, supporting infantry.

Injured soldiers were treated at Red Cross hospitals in Jury Street, Guy's Cliffe House and a 'recovery hospital' at Budbrooke Barracks. The largest of the hospitals was Hill House, off the Birmingham Road, overlooking the racecourse. Hill House opened in August 1915 with twenty beds and by the time it closed in March 1919 it had 120 beds, with 100 staff, many of them volunteers. Warwick also gave aid to soldiers from other countries, welcoming more than 200 refugees from Belgium by the end of 1915.

Social, political and economic chaos followed in the wake of the First World War. *Warwick in the Great War* records that many businesses soon experienced financial problems. Some goods were already in short supply and other traders demanded cash with orders. Employers of domestic servants either cut down or dispensed with them entirely.

Food shortages saw the establishment of the Warwickshire War Agricultural Committee in 1916 and the Women's Land Army was started in March 1916. As food shortages began to bite Warwick Borough Council insisted that all available uncultivated land in the borough should be used for food production. The Council turned a field in nearby Barford into allotments and this was later followed with other land being made available for allotments. To help feed the poor a national soup kitchen was set up in the borough.

As men left to join the forces, women, who had previously been confined to working in service, teaching or nursing, were needed to fill their roles on the home front. When the men returned after the war, they expected to resume their former roles in the workplace; however, women were not for giving up their jobs, leading to widespread protests on both sides.

Their roles in the war effort countrywide were however recognised by Parliament, resulting in the passing of the Representation of the People Act 1918. This allowed women over thirty years who met a property qualification to vote. Although 8.5 million women met this criterion, it was only around two-thirds of the total population of the United Kingdom. It wasn't until the passing of the Equal Franchise Act 1928 that women over the age of twenty-one were able to vote.

To commemorate the fallen, a war memorial was unveiled in 1921 before a large crowd. This was an Eleanor Cross spire featuring carved symbols of Warwickshire and is located by St Mary's churchyard railings where casualty lists were posted during the First World War.

After the Great War, which witnessed many maimed soldiers returning to 'civvy street', the veterans were obliged to earn a crust in any way they were able. In Warwick one enterprising veteran who had lost both legs on the Somme constructed a cart on which he sat mounted with sizeable lengths of blocks of salt. By this method he propelled himself around the town and would saw off a piece of salt for housewives at a penny per inch. Another disabled veteran acted as a horse-racing tipster and when the races were not on, he stood outside a pub with his bowler hat turned upside down and played a tin whistle.

Although the war years had taken its toll with loss of lives and food shortages, the town recovered and new manufacturing companies were established together with shops for provisions. The Great Depression following the Wall Street Crash in the United States in 1929 did not impact Warwick as much as in other parts of the country, notably the steel manufacturing industries in the north and mining in South Wales.

Industries in Warwick and Warwickshire, although feeling the effects of world depression in trade, were still flourishing. In January 1931, a speaker at the Annual Dinner of Engineering Employers and Staff said:

> That all those that revelled in the glories and antiquities of old Warwick, the beauties of the countryside and romance and history of Leamington, would do well to remind themselves of the industrial activities of the district. A casual glance at the list of the members of the Engineering Employers Association revealed the fact that a wide scope of industry was covered and in this area grates and stoves, wireless sets, motor-car bodies, piston rings, pumps and foodstuffs were made.

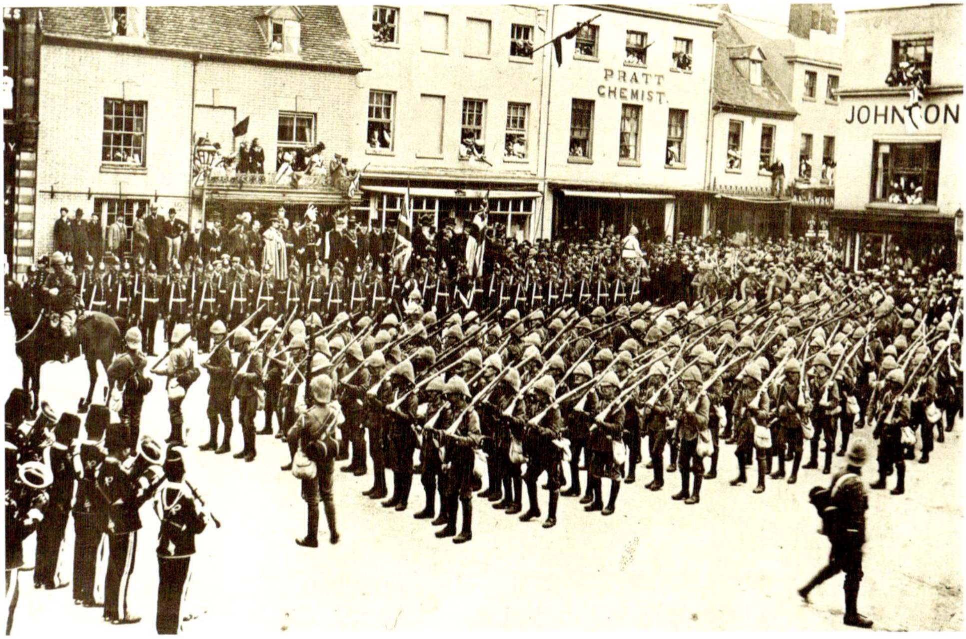

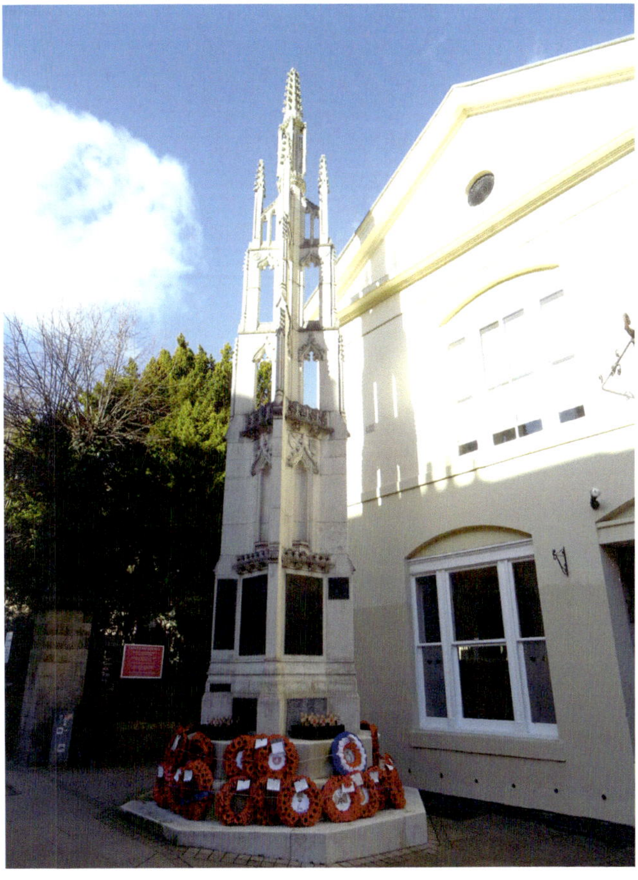

Above: The 6th Battalion of the Royal Warwickshire Regiment in the Market Place. (Image author's collection)

Right: The Eleanor Cross spire to commemorate the fallen, unveiled in 1921.

Other industry included the construction of new railway sidings for the Great Western Railway at Cape Road at a cost of £8,400.

Businesses included Hatton's and Wrights clothing stores in the Market Place. Other businesses in the Market Place were Carter Bros millinery; H. H. Collins, butchers; and A. B. Wylie, ironmongers. The Dale Hotel and Maunds Music Stores were situated in Old Square, Lacy, Printers in High Street, and Arthur Baker, ironmongers, and Onions shoe shop in Smith Street. Mr Matthew Bennett was advertised as a bone setter at Emscote Lodge.

Despite flourishing industries and businesses, there was still an economic and social impact on the town's people. The *Warwick & Warwickshire Advertiser* in 1931 records that on Christmas Day, ninety poor people obtained meals at the Soup Kitchen opened by George Nelson Dale at their works canteen. The Soup Kitchen, which had been opened for a week, showed ample evidence of its great need. Most of the bread and soup meals provided were collected by women and children for home consumption. One man visiting the kitchen said he had six children including a two-day-old baby and it was the thirteenth Christmas in succession he had been out of work. He was a painter and decorator by trade. Approximately fifty families each averaging six people were being helped daily.

Christmas festivities were abundant in the infirmary and children's homes with decorations, special meals and presents. The women's ward in the infirmary was decorated with a jolly representation of Warwick Mop on top of the stove, and a working model of a switchback. A carnival ball featured as the centrepiece of the men's ward. At the children's home in Linen Street the children were given presents and a splendid dinner of pork with apple sauce, plum pudding with sauce, mince pies and fruit. The children's home in Wharf Street provided stockings containing toys, hats, handkerchiefs, drawing sets and sweets.

Needs of the poor were met in various ways. In 1935 local resident Ron Kent recalls being taken to the Co-Op in Smith Street by his mother who purchased trousers, shirt, and sports jacket for him and his brother with dividends she had saved. These were to be worn on special occasions only. He also recalls a visit to the Cinderella Charity at the Court House where new boots for boys were issued.

Labourers fortunate enough to find work adopted a system of 'subbing'. Monday would see a queue at 'Uncles', the local pawnshop, where wives would take their husband's best suit to get a few coppers for Monday's meals. These would be redeemed the following Saturday in time for church Sunday evening. Contractors employing good labourers would insist on the daily 'subbing' knowing from experience that if the men were paid a whole week's wages, they would be lucky if they were even sober by Monday let alone turn up for work!

The official Town Guide of 1935 gives engineering, confectionery and gelatine production, motor-body building and agricultural implements manufacture as the principal industrial activities in the town. These manufacturers included George Nelson Dale, Wallwin (Pumps) and William Glover & Sons.

Shops abounded in the Market Square including clothing shops such as Hatton's for women and Wright's for men. Provision shops were provided by bakers, greengrocers, fish merchants, and sweet shops that lined the adjoining streets. These included

Walkers Stores, Melias, Rawsons, Plowmans, the Co-Op, Pearkes, Thacker & Christmas, International, Masons and Maypole in Smith Street and Ellis & Horne in Coten-End. Motor vehicles were few, with greengrocers, bakers, coal merchants and milkmen using horse and carts. Parcels were sent and received by the Stratford Blue bus which did a tour of the villages between Warwick and Stratford-upon-Avon.

Housing of some residents still proved a problem for the Borough Council. An overcrowding survey undertaken in 1935 found that 115 houses came into that definition, of which eighty had been remedied by moving the occupants to larger houses.

Demolition of the prison on Cape Road in 1933 made way for a new development of houses. These were built in the 1940s and saw the creation of Hanworth and Landor Roads. The Governor's House was all that remained of the prison and was to later become a public house and after it closed, offices and flats later still.

A country-wide food crisis in September 1938 had its impact in Warwick. Causes of the crisis were cited as the construction of large aerodromes, while road-widening schemes had taken up much land. The *Warwick & Warwickshire Advertiser* records that in Warwickshire alone 1,500 acres had been lost to cultivation because of one or other of these causes in the last three years.

The poor continued to have their medical needs met by Warwick Dispensary. It was recorded that in the year 1938 it had dealt with 3,200 patients, with 7,000 away from the dispensary. A total of 1,000 patients made urgent calls for medical attention outside dispensary hours. At its annual meeting in March 1939, The Warwick Provident Dispensary called for more subscriptions to enable its needs to be met.

Realisation that the country needed to be put on a war footing saw Warwick's Mayor, Alderman J. Allman, calling for volunteers for the armed services and fire services in February 1939. Most of the new recruits entered the Territorial Army. These included Ron Kent who had persuaded his mother to sign the form enabling him to join up despite being underage.

The Special Reserve of Battalions of the Royal Warwickshire Regiment was mobilised in August 1939 and four steam trains were provided for this purpose. As each train left the station, they were hailed with loud cheers from the huge crowd that had gathered in the coal-yard in Cape Road to see them off. Hats, hands and handkerchiefs were waved wildly.

In preparation for the war the priceless stained-glass windows in the Beauchamp Chapel of St Mary's were removed to be stored safely, and sandbags were placed around the tomb and effigy of Richard Beauchamp.

As a contribution to the war effort, Lord Warwick offered to have fifty evacuees at Warwick Castle in the event of an emergency, provided their care and supervision would be taken care of. Charles Guy Fulke Greville was also to become an active political figure after the war, becoming Mayor of Warwick between 1950 and 1951. During the 1950s he supported Anthony Eden in his campaign to become Prime Minister.

As an aspiring film actor, the earl was signed up with MGM to feature in *Dawn Patrol* with Errol Flynn and David Niven under the name of Michael Brooke. Unfortunately, he failed to cut the mustard as an actor and this was his one and only film.

PART III

Post-war to the Present – A Flourishing County and Market Town

The post-war years are the most significant in the history of Warwick since it was rebuilt following the Great Fire of 1694. Although the Industrial Revolution witnessed the expansion of Warwick as an industrial and commercial town and development as a county town, it was the Second World War which acted as a catalyst of major change in its history. Since 1945, political, economic, social, demographic and architectural influences have had a significant impact on the physical landscape. Up until the post-war years the urban density had remained compact and contained around Warwick's historic centre, surrounded by fields, common land, park land and farmland.

The boundaries of Warwick were first described briefly in 1554 and said to be the ancient boundaries of the town. The limits were shown as being Emscote Bridge in the

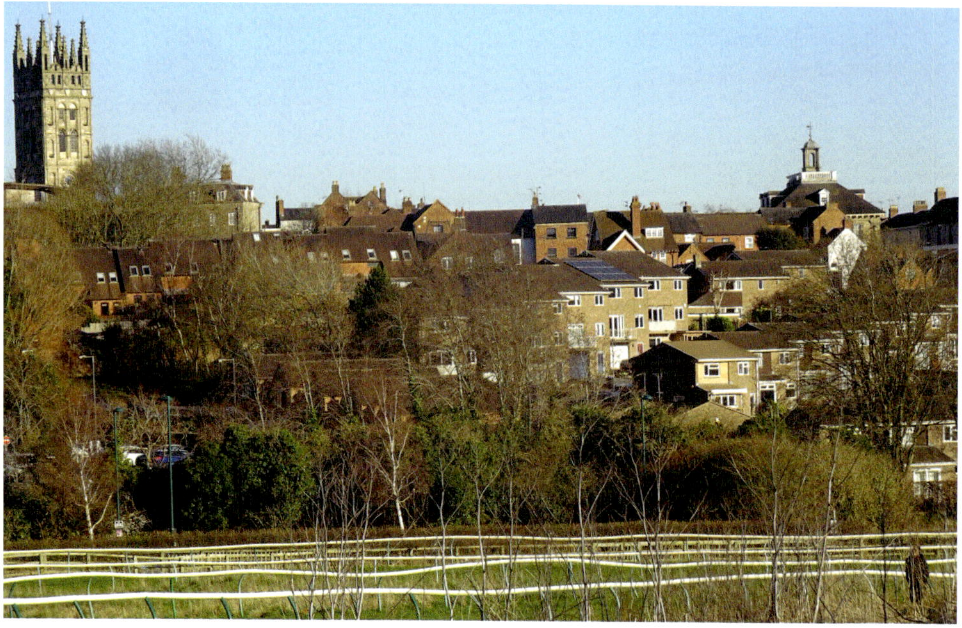

Warwick town beyond the racecourse. Once the town was compact and contained, surrounded by fields, parkland and common land.

east, Ford Mill Brook (Tach Brook) in the south, the outer edge of Longbridge in the west and Hampton Brook (Gog Brook) in the north.

A small market, county town with a stable and slow-growing population, Warwick was overshadowed by its neighbour, the more fashionable and popular Regency spa town of Leamington. Its attraction as a major tourist town of some importance was yet to be exploited.

Warwick has undergone many changes since the Second World War. The town was fortunate not to experience the bombing which saw much damage wrought in the nearby city of Coventry and the historic town centre remains very much the same today as it did pre-war. However, surrounding streets have seen changes with the loss of some buildings and erection of new. The street pattern that forms the centre of historic Warwick has changed very little prior to the Great Fire of 1694, as shown by the 'Ground Plott of Warwick' drawn by W. Hollar *c.* 1630.

The nature of the town serving a population of approximately 15,200 in 1945 has changed considerably with the spread of urbanisation, industrialisation and loss of surrounding green belt land. Warwick's unique historical character as a surviving small market town perched on a knoll, fortified with its impressive castle and town walls, overlooking the River Avon, surrounded by farmland and parkland is in danger of being compromised with development.

The town escaped the ravages of war; however, many of the smaller terraced houses were seen as unfit for habitation. These had no inside bathroom with hot and cold running water. Baths were taken in tin tubs, usually weekly, in front of a coal/coke fire or in the scullery, under the dim light of the gas mantle. The 1951 census records that less than half of the population had a fixed bath (48 per cent) while only 19 per cent had piped water to the building. The toilets were located outside in a communal yard and shared because there were too few toilets to the number of households in that yard. Many families occupied one or two rooms only.

After the war factories used for producing armaments were asked to switch to producing prefabricated units as temporary accommodation for the thousands of servicemen being returned to civilian life. In Warwick to help address the shortage of suitable accommodation prefabs were erected on the Packmores Estate *c.* 1946.

Like other towns in Britain, the post-war situation presented the Borough Council with a challenge and an opportunity to make radical changes which would sweep away post-war austerity and revolutionise people's living conditions and lifestyles. Driven by a need to improve public health, a post-war programme of slum clearance was embarked upon that rid the town of many communal yards, outside water standpipes and shared lavatories.

To accommodate those displaced by the slum clearance programme and also an expanding population, planning for the housing, industrial, agricultural, educational and recreational needs for Warwick both present and future had to be looked at with due regard for its historical character as a county and small market town. It was against this background in 1950 that Sir Patrick Abercrombie's report on the planning for Warwick for the next fifty years was considered by a special meeting of the Housing Committee. Its adoption was proposed together with recommendations that the probable increase in the population in the borough over the next fifty years be limited to a maximum of 20,000.

The aim of the *Abercrombie Plan for Warwick* was to maintain it as the paramount historic asset of the Midlands and eventually to make it a cultural centre of the area. It proposed that the long-term aim of piecemeal construction should be to preserve as far as possible the historical character of the area; to reduce the density of development in those parts of the area which are at present overcrowded; to reduce the number of shops and other buildings which attract a large volume of traffic; to accentuate the natural possibilities of the site and to provide a space for car parks, local open spaces and improved access to buildings.

A structure plan for Warwick district 1996–2004 set a target of 8,000 houses to be built by the end of 2004. The numbers of houses built and committed were 9,173.

A speaker at the Warwick Society's Annual Meeting in 1958 highlighted the fact that the town was on the eve of changes possibly as great as any since the borough was rebuilt after the Great Fire of 1694, in a manner that had commanded the admiration of every generation since. Slum clearance, street widening, possible industrial development on the outskirts of town and further street lighting schemes showed that Warwick had reached a stage in its development that called for the most careful thought and planning.

Commenting on post-war changes, Richard K. Morris in *Buildings of Warwick* said that some of these had been regrettable, particularly mainly around the Market Square, which until the 1950s he describes as a proper country town square, being a wide-open space. The Square was virtually surrounded by two- and three-storey houses with the

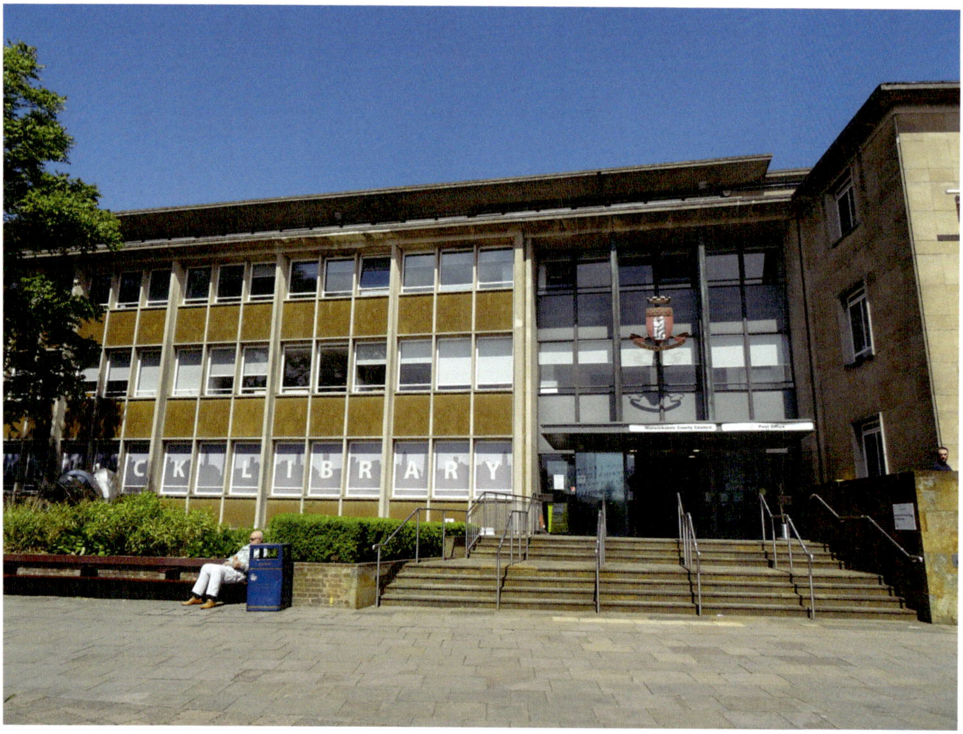

The Shire Hall, Market Place. The extension to the Shire Hall was built in the 1960s and formally opened by the Queen Mother in 1966.

Market House to the south being the only larger building. The buildings at the north end were demolished at the end of the 1950s to make way for an extension to the Shire Hall and an access road by Abbotsford House. He also criticises the wholesale redevelopment of Market Street which he describes as 'in a bland, untidy and confused late 1960s manner'.

Proposed plans included for development behind St Paul's Church in Bread and Meat Close and on Lammas fields. Captain E. G. Tibbits wrote on post-war housing in Warwick:

> The common is and has been a source of pleasure and health to hundreds of Warwick children and their parents and I fear once the process of whittling away parts of the common commences it will be continued.

Some development was successfully opposed, like Hill Close Gardens off Linen Street. These were part of the Marble House estate in 1788. The area was enclosed in 1845 to provide a place for relaxation for shopkeepers and others living over town-centre premises. The area was divided into twenty-four plots and owners and tenants would visit the gardens on Sundays to tend their fruit and vegetables. A suggested development of up to fifty houses was opposed by the Lammas and District Resident's Association and English Heritage.

Hill Close Gardens have now been preserved as an important part of Warwick's history. A programme to restore the unique Victorian gardens and summerhouses was embarked upon and these are now open to the public.

Hill Close Gardens was also the site of part of a project to install and activate several environmentally friendly wind turbines. These were installed in February 2007 to assess the practicality of getting more sustainable energy sources. Other designated sites were the Princes Drive Recycling Centre and a Leamington resident's home. The aim of Warwick Microwind trial was to evaluate the contribution rooftop-mounted wind turbines may make in improving the energy performance of existing homes in Warwick and nationally.

The Abercrombie Plan included for the development of corporation housing to be built on sites to the south-west and north-east of the town. In the early 1950s construction commenced on the Forbes Estate built on land between the Stratford Road and Hampton Road, and later the Percy Estate to the north-east. The Percy Estate was designed to create in Warwick one of the most modern municipal housing sites in the Midlands. Jackson & Edmonds were consulting architects for the estate, the erection of which commenced in 1957.

By 1960 council house building in Warwick had outstripped private building by nearly 4:1 since 1945. The new council houses built complied with the Parker Morris space standards which stated that space should be made available for typical items of furniture and space needed to move around it. Although the recommendations were not made mandatory until 1969 for council housing, these had mostly been implemented in Warwick by then. Council houses built on the Forbes Estate between Hampton Road and Stratford Road also had sizeable gardens. This saw a substantial transformation from the cramped living conditions of yesteryear and rise in living standards.

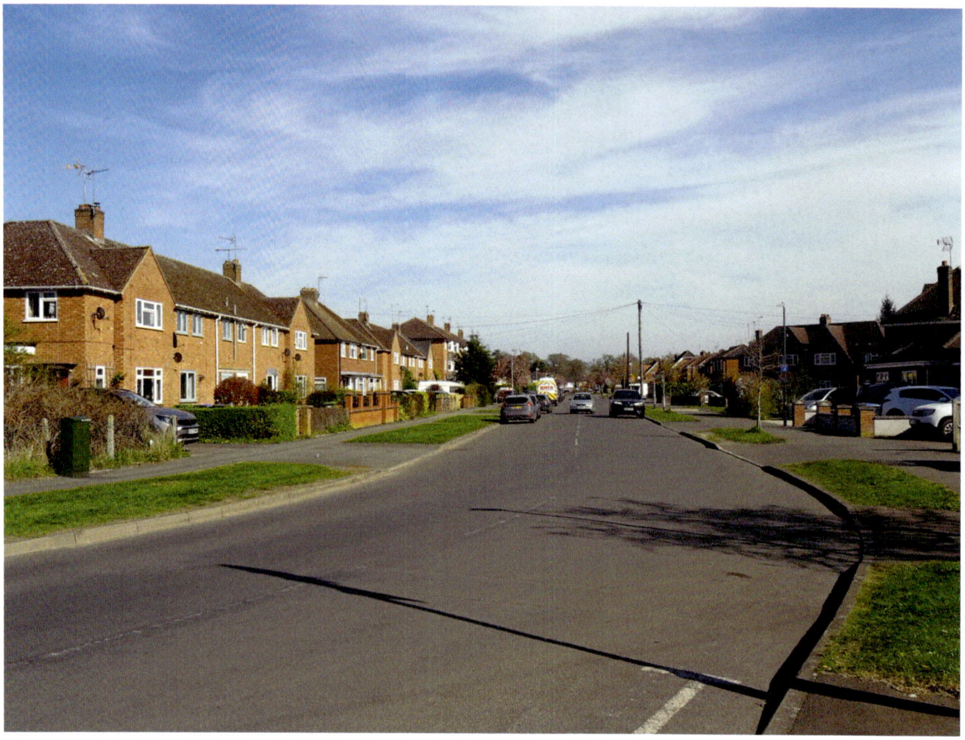

Forbes Estate was built on open land between Hampton Road and Stratford Road in the 1950s to accommodate those displaced by the wholesale 'slum' clearances.

Warwick Town Council replaced Warwick Borough Council in 1974, resulting from local government reorganisation. This dealt a substantive blow to the autonomy of the former Borough Council which saw the Municipal Borough and Rural District amalgamation with Leamington to form Warwick District Council. This meant a major loss of powers for the Council, although it retained its status as a town with its own mayor. Effectively reduced to a parish council, decisions affecting the development of Warwick could now only be recommended to the District Council.

With development continuing apace, there was a danger that the intrinsic historical nature of the town could be compromised. A report produced by Harold Mytum in 1975 highlighted Warwick as a town of major historical and archaeological importance having undergone a considerable amount of modern development. He pointed out that modern building techniques often destroy all archaeological deposits and emphasised the importance of the allied discipline of architecture where the examination of standing buildings can add to our understanding of history.

An example of destruction and modern development (not altogether pleasing) was the demolition of Brook House in 1960 and erection of a row of shops with flats above at St John's/Coventry Road. Proposals to demolish Brook House on the Coventry Road and build shops and flats in the garden of The Brook were carried out despite objections from the Warwick Society. They had argued that the area incorporating the Crown Hotel,

St, John's House and the group of houses leading into St Nicholas Church Street remained an impressive outpost of the historic centre of Warwick.

The Brook was included in the schedule of buildings considered to be of historical and architectural importance. Sir Edward Ford, secretary of the Pilgrim Trust, urged local authorities to take the long view and realise they were only temporary trustees of historic towns like Warwick.

Warwick Society was praised for its successful efforts to preserve buildings such as the former Bear and Baculus Public House on the corner of High Street and Brook Street. The Bear and Baculus closed for business in September 1970 and is now in private ownership. A row of listed cottages in the Saltisford, formerly owned by Hestair Eagle Limited, were demolished and replaced by a three-storey office block in approximately 1981. A three-storey block of twenty flats replaced St Mary's Hall in The Butts. This had been previously used as a classroom by the King's High School for Girls. Opposing the demolition, the Ancient Monuments Society described the building as 'eccentric but much for more arresting than the block of proposed flats'.

Economic and social influences had a significant impact on the physical landscape of Warwick. In early 1957 Warwick businesses were affected by serious fuel restrictions and credit squeeze in the Middle East which resulted in redundancies and the introduction of a four-day week. In 1960 the situation had been reversed and a wave of prosperity experienced by most firms in Warwick brought its own problems such as lack of space for expansion.

Subsequently the land at Wedgnock beyond the canal, zoned as a green belt area by the County Council but opposed by the Town Council, was bought through the Castle Estates sale by Eagle Engineering and Wallwin (Pumps) Limited, both having premises in

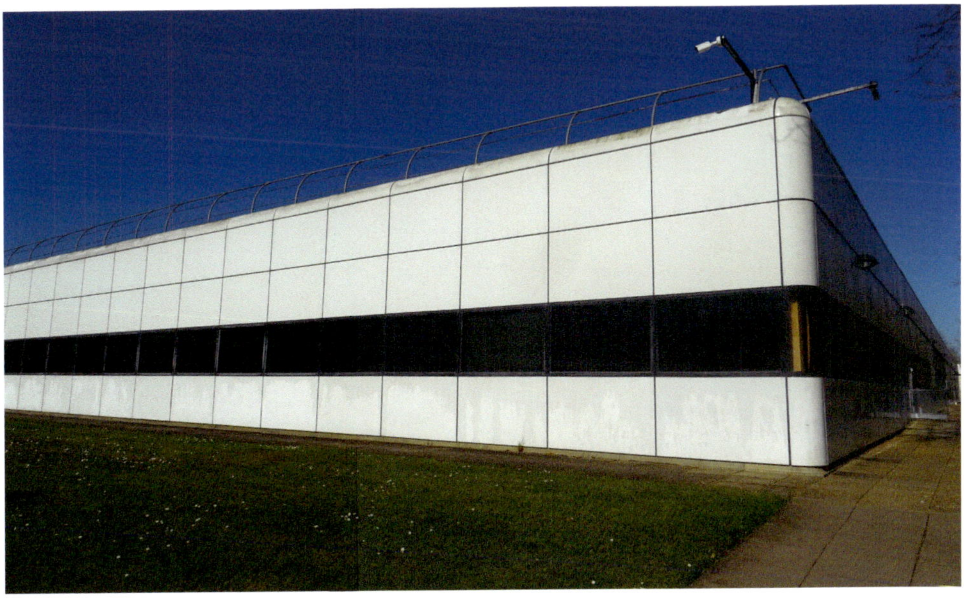

The premises of IBM cover 35 acres which encompassed the nursery farm of pig farmer Ken Payne. Plans for its construction were submitted in 1975.

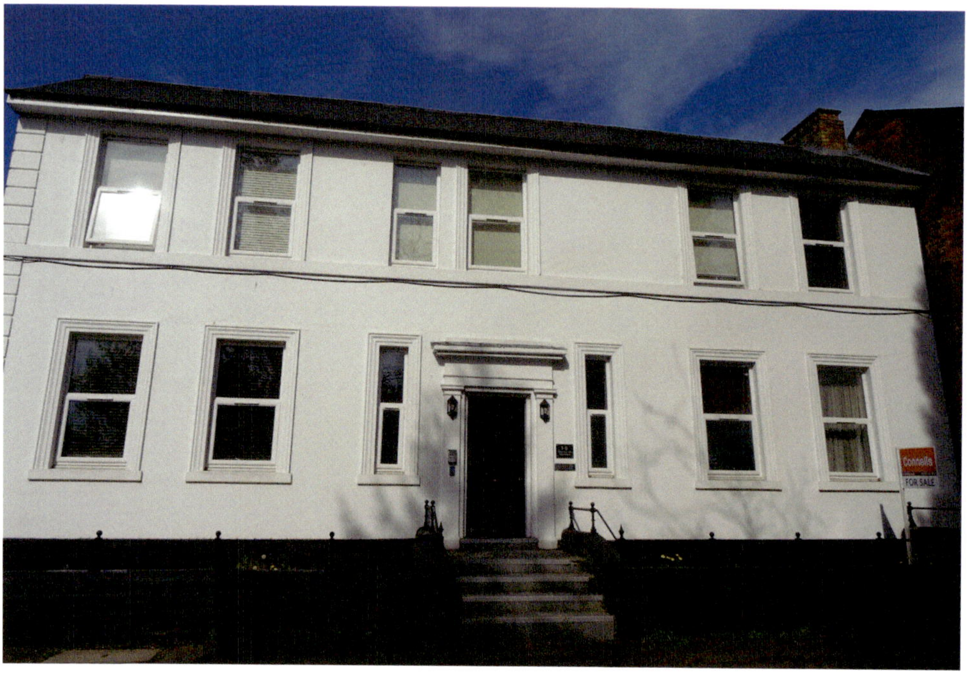

Former offices of George Nelson Dale, manufacturers of gelatine and isinglass, established in 1837. The business closed in 1969.

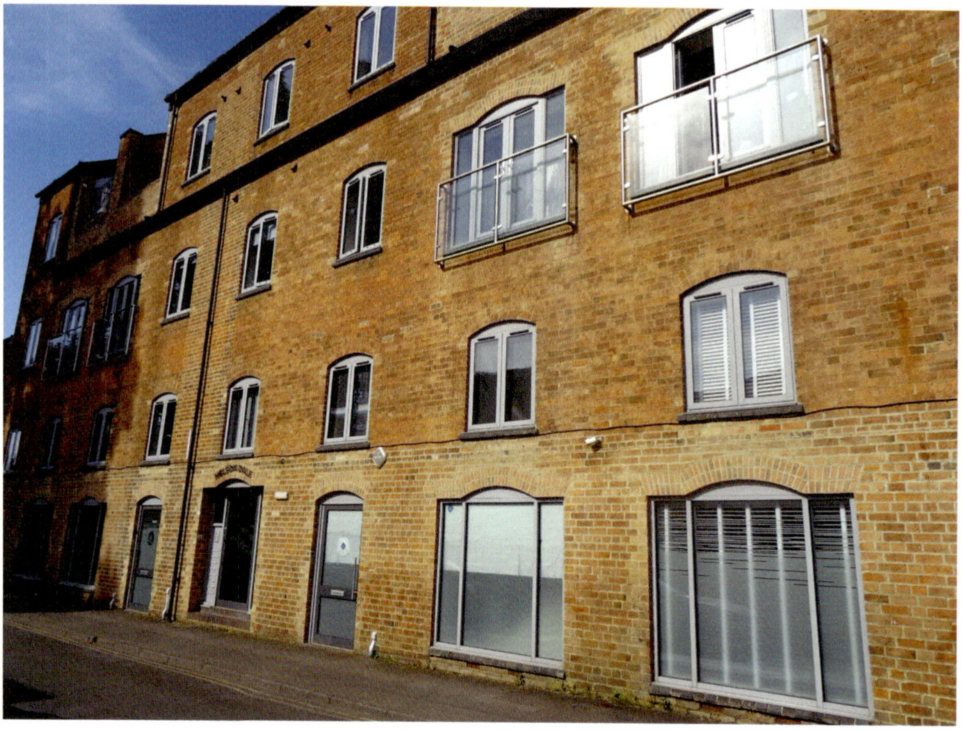

Former factory buildings of George Nelson Dale in Wharf Street.

the Saltisford. Three acres of land formerly owned by Kench's Flour Mill on the Emscote Road and used as allotments since the First World War was bought by Warwick Town Council for £6,000.

The oil crises of 1973 affected many firms in Warwick, which again saw redundancies and reduction of working days. Despite these problems expansion continued and led to new technology firms such as IBM establishing a base in Warwick. These submitted plans in January 1975 to build the massive office complex covering 35 acres, off the Birmingham Road, also encompassing the old nursery farm owned by local pig farmer Ken Payne.

New technology businesses saw greater employment opportunities for the local and wider community; however, this meant a change in the skills base to more hi-tech. Manufacturing businesses had started to decline. One of the oldest family firms in Warwick and an employer of many Warwick people, George Nelson Dale, gelatine and isinglass manufacturers, closed at the end of 1969. It was first established in 1837 in Leamington Spa and moved to Warwick in 1845. The buildings were described as typical of the late Industrial Revolution and built around 1900. These were later demolished and replaced with modern industrial buildings.

A surviving family firm, Frederick Freer, was originally situated in Smith Street and later relocated to West Street. It was founded in 1836 by Frederick Freer, seller of canvas goods, flags and bunting. The business moved to Emscote Mills in Wharf Street in 1999.

Expansion of Warwick and its geographical location as a through route for traffic led to problems of congestion. It was proposed that an inner-relief road was to take through traffic on a route that did not conflict with traffic using the town and to protect the historic centre of Warwick. Plans for the controversial inner-relief road were abandoned by members of Warwick Town Council at a special General Purposes Committee meeting in 1970. It was stated that the road was unnecessary considering the proposed development north of the canal and Leamington's plan for a western relief road and would be a waste of public money.

A thriving county town steeped in history, Warwick is also home to many customs and traditions, some of which have survived and others now defunct. The changing face of Warwick witnessed the demise of the customary Assizes and Quarter Sessions in 1972 which was replaced by the Crown Courts. It was seen that it was unlikely for High Court judges to sit at the Shire Hall in future, therefore breaking the custom going back over centuries which saw judges attending the preliminary service at St Mary's and being greeted by buglers.

The horse fair, traditionally held on the second Monday in November on the Back Hills (Castle Hill) where horse traders bought and sold horses/ponies, has also ceased. Other changes saw the alteration of churches to reflect dwindling congregations. This was bitterly opposed by some as the church was in earlier times a cornerstone of the community. A letter sent to the *Warwickshire & Warwick Advertiser* by a resident of the parish of St Paul's on its proposed alteration stated: 'If you take away our church you will take part of our lives with it. Most of us have been born and brought up in St. Paul's parish and to us it is home.'

The annual event of the Mop is held in October, a centuries-old tradition that continues to this day. The site of the Mop has also attracted controversy; however, this time-honoured

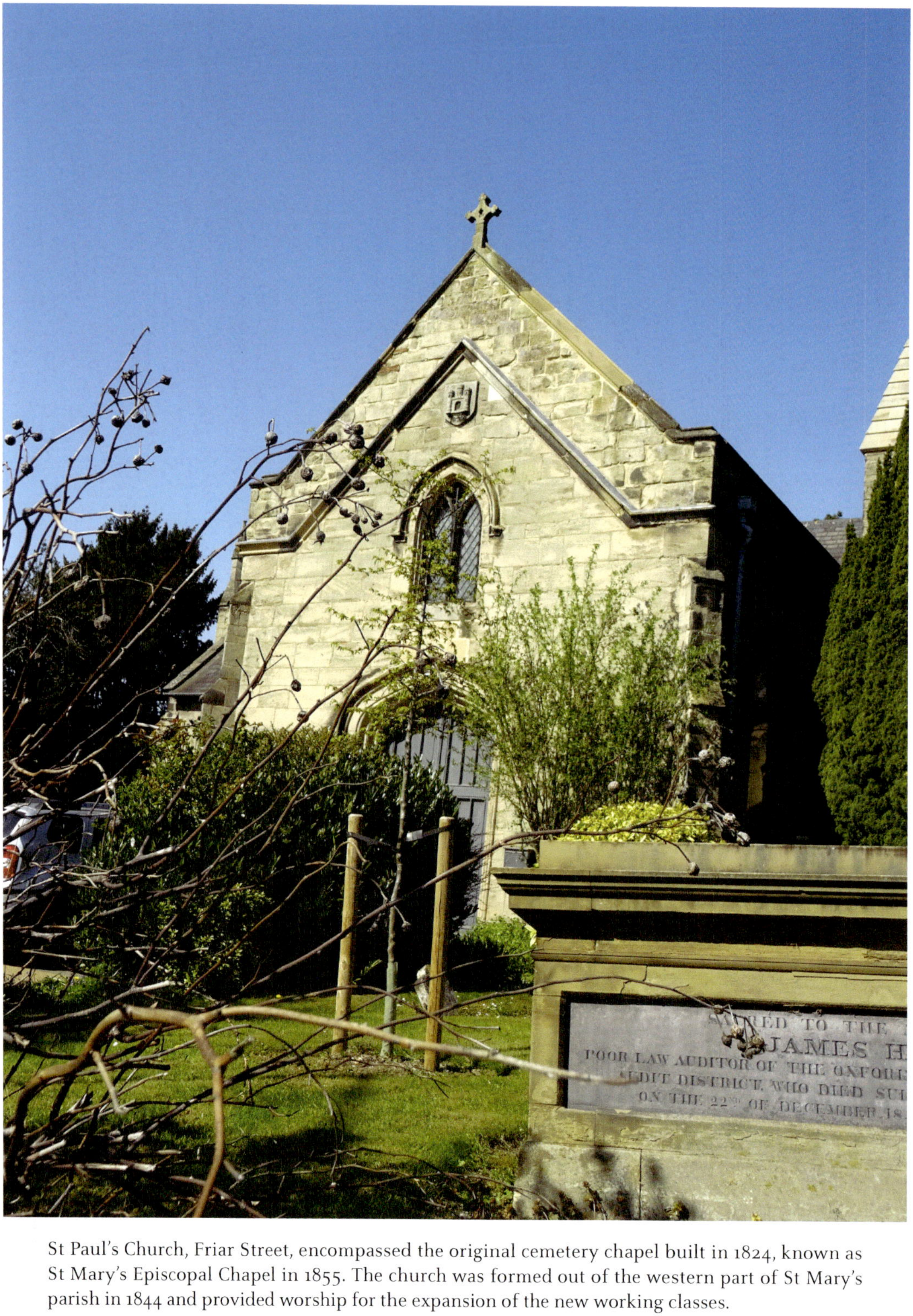

St Paul's Church, Friar Street, encompassed the original cemetery chapel built in 1824, known as St Mary's Episcopal Chapel in 1855. The church was formed out of the western part of St Mary's parish in 1844 and provided worship for the expansion of the new working classes.

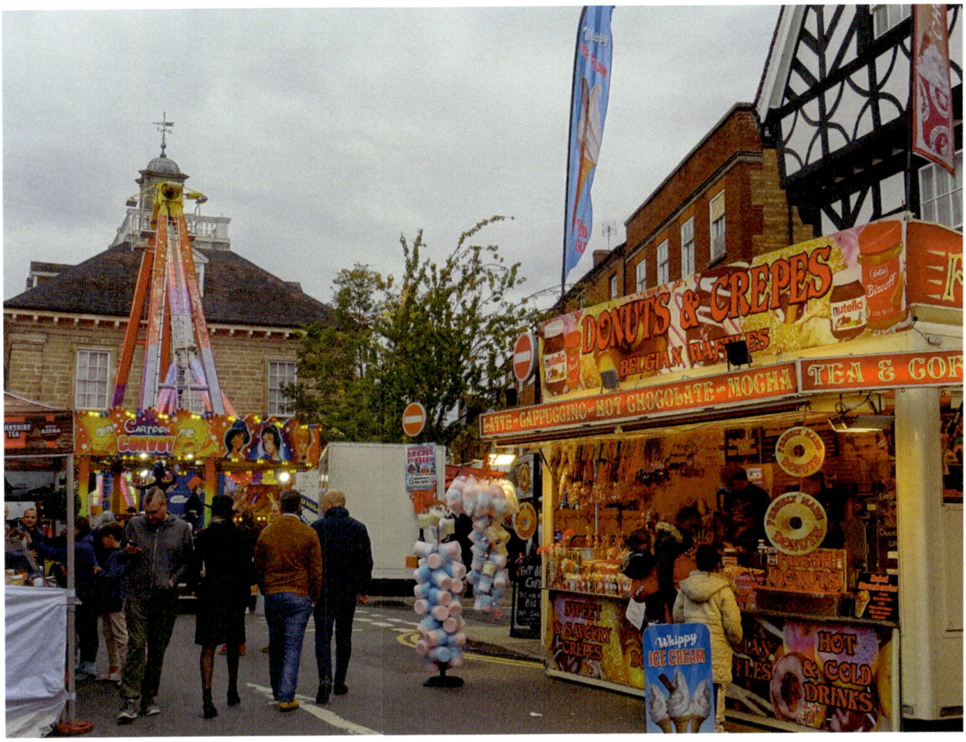

Warwick Mop has a long tradition. A fair for eight days toll free was first established by Earl John du Plessis in the thirteenth century.

custom continues to take its traditional place in the Market Square despite efforts by the District Council to relocate it to the racecourse. The custom of people hiring themselves out as servants and labourers has long since disappeared, reflecting the changes in society from being in service to that of an employee. These days it is operated as a Mop Fair with stalls and roundabouts only. It was cancelled in October 1950 because the Showmen's Guild refused to agree to the increased Mop tolls of fourpence halfpenny per square foot introduced by Warwick Corporation. Many letters of complaint were received by the Borough Council from local people, and the matter was later resolved to allow the tradition to continue.

Warwick is also a market town and has its origins in a Charter by Philip and Mary in 1554. Tuesday and Saturday were the appointed market days. The livestock market was held more recently on Wednesday on the site to the rear of St John's Court and ceased during the 1970s. The sales of sheep, cattle and horses had previously been restricted to Brook Street in the latter half of the nineteenth century. A market of stalls selling household goods, clothing and fruit and vegetables continues to be held in the Market Place on Saturday. Farmers and French markets have become a more recent popular feature and are held sporadically also in the Market Place.

More recently new customs have come into being. Carols at the Castle has been an annual event held in December since the 1970s and attracts many visitors. The highly popular custom is held in the courtyard, with glowing braziers relieving the darkness,

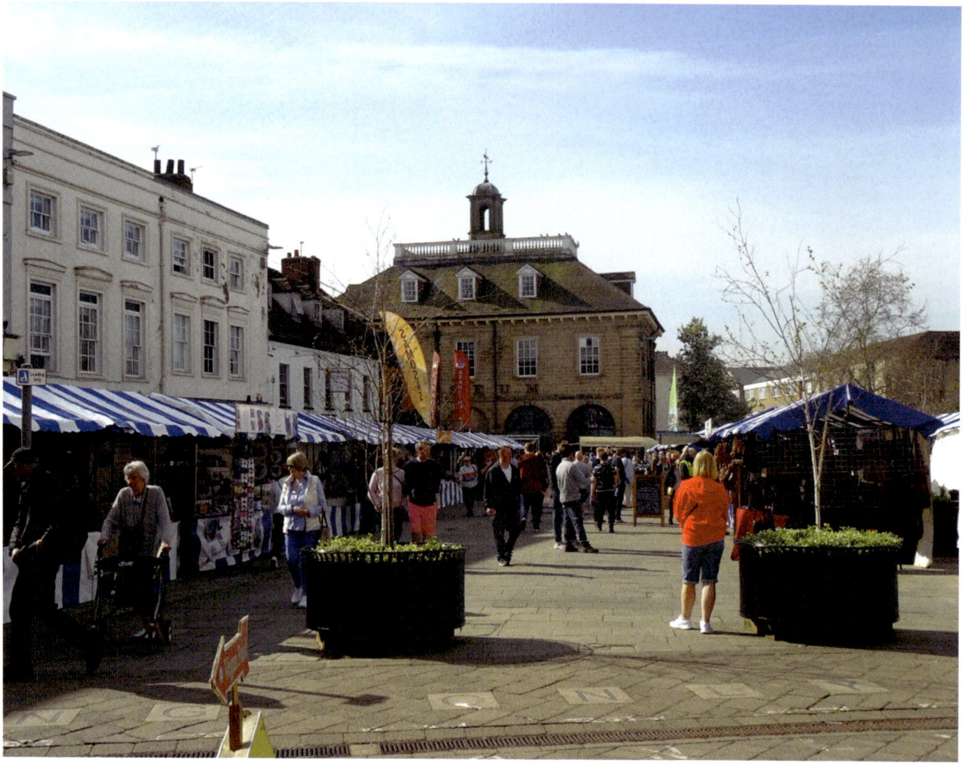

Warwick Market has its origins in a Statute of Philip and Mary, 1554.

and is wonderfully atmospheric. In common with other towns in Britain, Warwick also plays host to the Victorian Fair in November/December and gives much pleasure to locals and visitors alike.

Without question the most outstanding aspect of Warwick's activities is that of a tourist centre. The town's ability to adapt to social and industrial changes has maintained Warwick as part of an affluent economic belt encompassing Stratford-upon-Avon and Royal Leamington Spa.

The population has undergone socio-economic changes which have lifted the majority out of relative poverty in line with the rest of Britain, due initially to the implementation of the Welfare State in 1948. In 1945 many local people worked and lived on the same premises, while others worked for local firms. Transport was mainly by foot, bicycle, bus and train. Car ownership was very limited until the 1950s. Rationing continued until the early 1950s. Extended families where two or three generations lived either with or in close proximity to their kith and kin were the norm.

The census shows that the population in 1951 was 15,349. By 2001 this had grown to 25,931, an increase over fifty years of 59 per cent. Of these 62 per cent were making the journey to work by car or van, indicating that people were now travelling further to their place of work and this was the preferred or necessary mode of travel. Less than 5 per cent were choosing to travel by train or bus and 13 per cent were on foot.

Population growth continues to occur most rapidly in South Warwickshire. Nearly half of the 2004–05 population growth in the county has taken place in Warwick district and the area continues to experience the greatest rate of growth, attracting significant levels of inward migration which has contributed to an almost 3 per cent increase over this period.

Expansion of Warwick and growing affluence of society has witnessed the transition from extended to nuclear families, single people and a new breed of commuters. This is reflected in the housing stock which also marks a transition from social housing to home ownership and rental through private landlords who buy to let. Contributing to this phenomenon was the Thatcher Right to Buy scheme in the 1980s which enabled council house tenants to purchase their properties at a discount. In 2001 housing occupancy was 73 per cent with 14 per cent renting from the local authority and 7 per cent renting from private landlords.

Many newcomers to Warwick have decided to live in what is regarded as a green, leafy and pleasant environment while working in major cities and this has been made possible by the construction of the M40 in the 1980s linking Warwick with London and the new Parkway station built at Stank's Farm in 2000. In 2022/23 the station was recorded as having had 377,132 entries and exits, making it the 889th most used station out of 2,575 stations in Great Britain. This has contributed to Warwick being a vibrant if somewhat mobile and transient society. No longer do we find many family members working for a

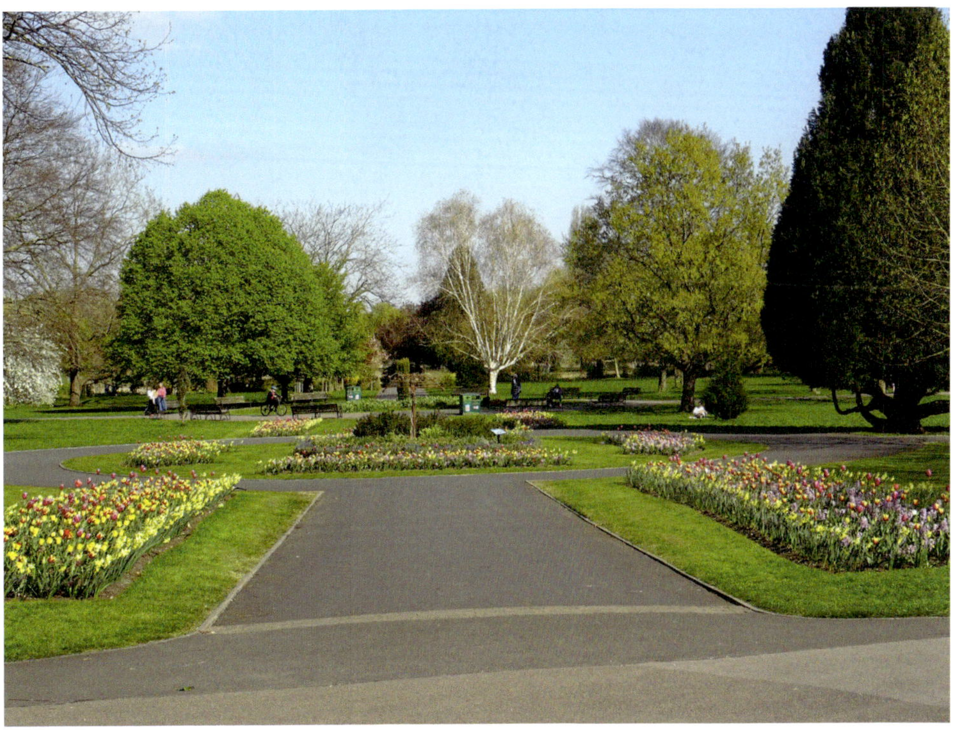

St Nicholas Park was established on St Nicholas Meadows in 1933.

family employee. A largely manufacturing-based industry in 1945 has been succeeded by largely service-based and administrative hubs.

Café society thrives in Warwick and reflects a more affluent era, attracting many younger people to the area. Smith Street, once the Jewish quarter and home to the goldsmiths and gunsmiths of Warwick, also to the poet and writer Walter Savage Landor in 1775, now bustles with many diverse independent businesses and restaurants.

New housing estates springing up in previously designated green belt areas surrounding the town also reflects growth and prosperity; however, this has had its critics. The development of the green belt land off Hampton Road/Gog Brook in the 1990s was bitterly opposed by a local councillor who declared it would ruin Warwick as a small, historic county town.

Although no longer having a resident earl, Warwick Castle continues to serve the town economically, attracting thousands of visitors each year and hosting events such as the summer music festival and Carols at the Castle. Vacated by its last incumbent, Lord

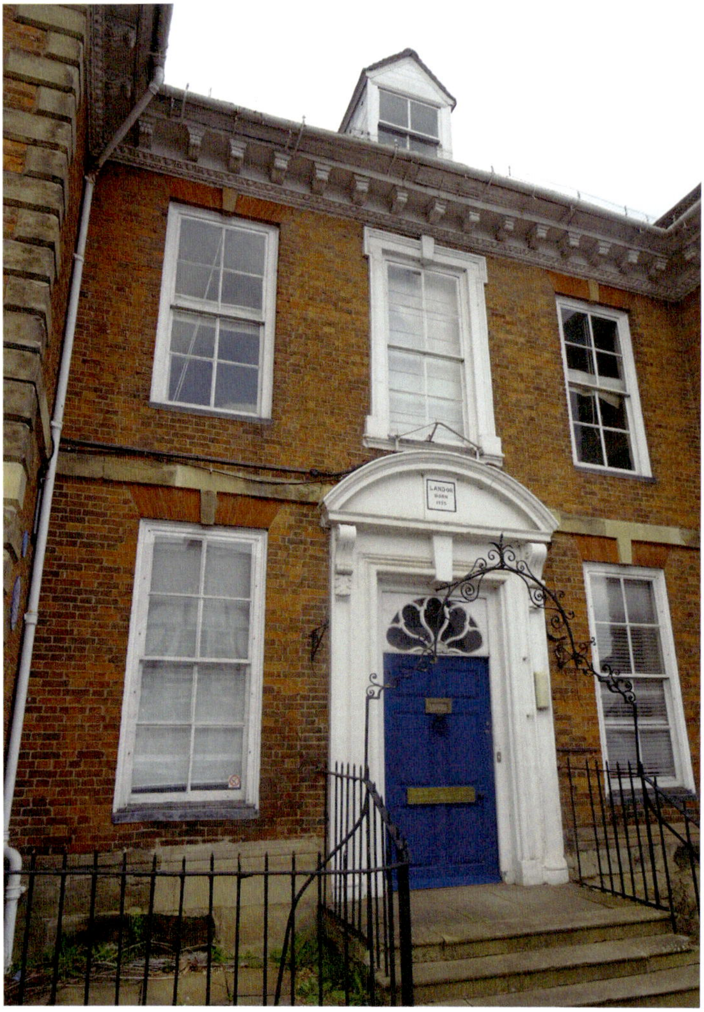

Landor House, built by Roger Hurlbut, 1692–3. This was the birthplace of Walter Savage Landor, poet and writer, 1775. During his school years he was described as a 'mad Jacobin' because of his outrageous mode of dress. He died in Florence, Italy, in 1864.

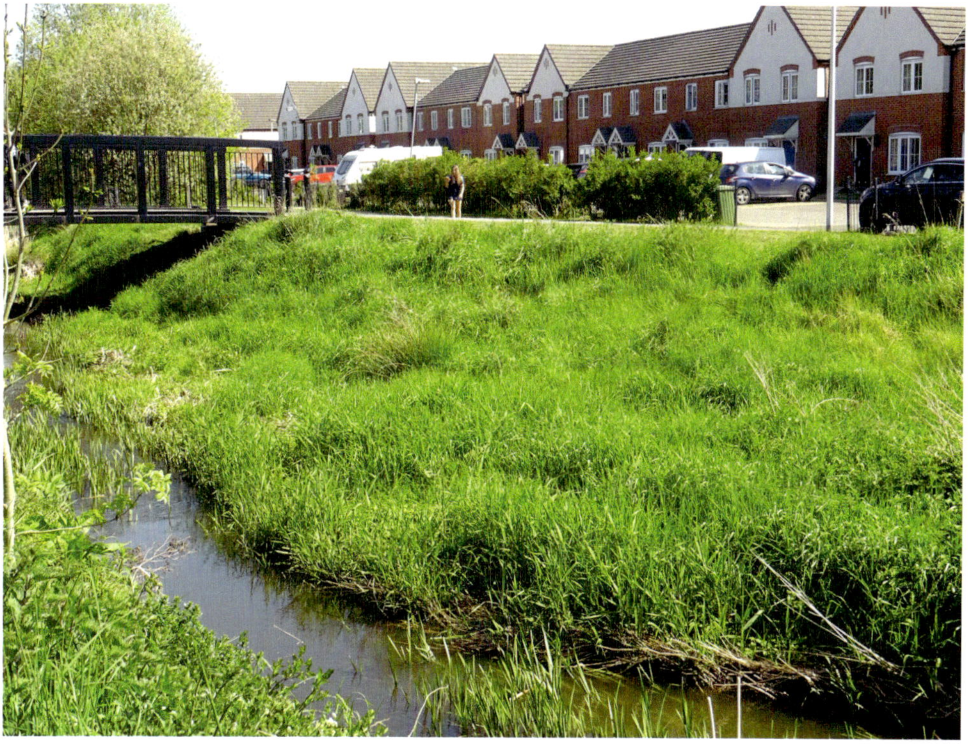

The Chase, built beyond Gog Brook (Hampton Brook) on green belt land to accommodate an expanding population. Building of the estate commenced in the 1990s. Gog Brook once formed the boundary to Warwick.

Brooke, who succeeded to the title of earl on his father's death in 1984, the castle was sold to Madame Tussauds in 1978.

The company established a series of waxworks exhibitions, among these a scene depicting the Kingmaker calling his men to arms, and a social gathering with Daisy, Countess of Warwick entertaining the Prince of Wales. The castle was taken over by Merlin Entertainments, the biggest theme park company in America in 2007, and they have added other attractions. These include the firing of the giant trebuchet (a medieval siege weapon), falconry displays, the haunting of the 'ghost tower' and children's entertainments.

From its humble beginnings, Warwick has progressed through the centuries, becoming a thriving, affluent market and county town. It has survived and prospered despite five major incidents: the Great Fire, the Civil War, a bank failure and two world wars. Initially defended by its castle, wall and gates and feudal lords, the rebuilding of the town after the Great Fire attracted professionals and gentry, contributing to Warwick's establishment as the administrative centre of the borough.

Manufacturing businesses such as George Nelson Dale, Cape Engineering (later Cape (Warwick) Holdings), and William Glover have been replaced with administrative services. Other major manufacturing businesses such as Wallwin Pumps (later Biwater), Dennis Eagle, The Improved Hinges and Benfords have relocated to sites elsewhere. The population has expanded and at the 2021 census was recorded as 31,955. Housing estates have been developed on the once green belt land to accommodate this influx; however, the centre of Warwick retains its historic character since it was rebuilt after the Great Fire of 1694 and continues to attract many tourists.

The occupations of its residents show a similarity with the eighteenth century, having a large demographic of professionals and managerial officials. However, in stark contrast the living conditions and housing of the poor have improved considerably since then. Affluence is reflected in the type of housing and lack of total deprivation. The 2021 census records that 57 per cent of households had no deprivation while 29.5 per cent were deprived in one area only.

Although having lost its civic autonomy through being incorporated in Warwick District Council, the town still retains its own mayor, which reflects its civic pride. The mayor of Warwick is a role steeped in tradition and ceremony. Since 1664 the mayor has been the first citizen of Warwick and represents the town with the insignia of the mace, robes and chains of office and connects the present day with history, acting as a symbol of continuity. In line with other towns in the country, Warwick established links with its counterparts Saumur, France, in 1989 and Verden, Germany, in 1994.

As stated by Philip B. Chatwin, author of *Old Warwick*:

> For it was never more important that in every old place and not least in Warwick itself a new pride of heritage should be born, a sense of the wealth around us recreated and a determination withal to see the best of the past preserved in our time for the enrichment of the world tomorrow.

Bibliography

A History of the County of Warwick, Vol. 2 (Originally published by Victoria County History, London, 1908)

A History of the County of Warwick, Vol. 8 – Stephens, W. B. (ed.) (Oxford University Press, 1969)

A History of Warwick and Its People – Kemp, Thomas (H. T. Cooke & Son, 1905)

A History of Warwick Hospital 1836-1903 – Holden, J. N.

A Medieval Potpourri – Blog at WordPress.com

A Visitor's Companion to Tudor England – Lipscombe, Suzannah (Edbury Press, 2012)

A Window on the History of St. Nicholas Church, the First 1,000 Years – Hamilton, Arthur (Friends of St Nicholas)

Alderson House – Collier, Frank (Archivist, Alderson House)

Anglo-Saxon Finds in Warwick – Chatwin Philip B. (Cambridge University Press, 2012)

Anglotopia Club – Author Jonathan

Antiquities of Warwickshire – Dugdale, William (London: Thomas Warren, 1656)

Archaeology – Gethin, Bryn, Palmer, Stuart C., Pratt, E. (Archaeology Warwick, 2011)

Around Warwick in Old Photographs – Booth, Rosemary (Alan Sutton Publishing Ltd, 1990)

Brooke's Battery – Spinks, Philip (Brewin Books, 2008)

Canaletto and Warwick Castle – Buttery, David (Phillimore & Co. Ltd, 1992)

GATEHOUSE: The comprehensive gazetteer and bibliography of medieval castles, fortifications and palaces of England, Wales and The Islands.

Glimpses of Our Local Past – Manning, J. C. (C. Forster, 1991)

Historic Warwick, Kemp, T.

Kings & Castles – Online

Old Warwick – Chatwin, Philip B. (Compton Dando, 1951)

'Our Warwickshire' – Online

The Black Book of Warwick – Edited and transcribed by Kemp, T. (ed. tr.) (Henry C. Cooke & Son)

The Book of Warwick – Lines, Charles (Barracuda Books Ltd, 1985)

The Buildings of Warwick – Morris, Richard K. & Hoverd, Ken (Alan Sutton Publishing Ltd, 1994)

The Damnation of John Donellan – Cooke, Elizabeth (Profile Books Ltd, 2011)

The Darling Daisy Affair – Lang Theo (New York Atheneum, 1966)

The History of Parliament – Escott, Margaret

The History of Parliament – Thorne, R. G.

The Past in Warwick: Tudors to Victorians –Alcock, Nat (ed.) (University of Warwick, 1985)

The Warwick Canals – Faulkner, Alan H. (Railway & Canal Historical Society, 1986)

Warwick & Warwickshire Advertiser
Warwick Castle (Warwick Castle Estates Office, 1953)
Warwick Castle and Its Earls: From Saxon Times to the Present Day – Evelyn Maynard, Countess of Warwick (Hutchinson & Co., 1903)
Warwick and Its People 1694-1730 – Yates, J. R. S. (Self-published)
Warwick Archaeology – Mytum, Harold (report)
Warwick in the Great War – Sutherland, G. (Amberley Publishing)
Warwick in Times Past – Gates, P. J. E. (Countryside Publications, 1982)
Warwick: Its Preservation & Redevelopment – Abercrombie P., Nickson R. (London: The Architectural Press, 1949)
Warwick Museum Timetrail – Farr, M. & Taylor, S.
Warwick the Kingmaker – Kendall, Paul M. (George Allen & Unwin Ltd, 1957)
Warwick Then & Now – Williams, Lynne (The History Press, 2012)
Warwick Town Council Official Guide (APP Ltd, January 1996)
World History Encyclopedia – Cartwright, Mark

Acknowledgements

I would like to thank the following for their valuable contributions:

Paul Williams, Leamington Spa Courier Series – Warwick & Warwickshire Advertiser, Rufus Dent (Lord Leycester), Veronica Brown for her father Ron Kent's memoirs, *Our Warwickshire*.

About the Author

Lynne Williams is a graduate of Warwick University where she studied the history of Europe, including the United Kingdom, Russia and Japan from the 1600s to modernity. Her interests are reading, walking and researching where she is fortunate to have a good archive office in Warwick. She is also well travelled, and favourite destinations include Switzerland and India.